*virtual*intimacies

*virtual*intimacies

MEDIA, AFFECT, AND QUEER SOCIALITY

Shaka McGlotten

Cover art by Rory Golden. Wood block print and laser printing over collage on paper. 10 inches × 7½ inches. © 2012 Rory Golden. Used with permission.

Published by
STATE UNIVERSITY OF NEW YORK PRESS, ALBANY

For information, contact
STATE UNIVERSITY OF NEW YORK PRESS, ALBANY, NY
www.sunypress.edu

Production, Laurie Searl
Marketing, Fran Keneston

Library of Congress Cataloging-in-Publication Data

McGlotten, Shaka, 1975–
    Virtual intimacies : media, affect, and queer sociality / Shaka McGlotten.
        pages cm
    Includes bibliographical references and index.
    ISBN 978-1-4384-4877-0 (hc : alk. paper) 978-1-4384-4878-7 (pb : alk. paper)
    1. Gay men—Sexual behavior.   2. Internet—Social aspects.   3. Interpersonal communication.
4. Computer networks—Social aspects.   I. Title.
    HQ76.25.M372 2013
    306.77086'642—dc23   2013000129

10 9 8 7 6 5 4 3 2 1

Contents

Acknowledgments

This book has been a lesson in sociality. I am grateful for the feedback and support of colleagues, who have modeled the criticality and care that supports every good friendship. Jason Pine, Agustin Zarzosa, Michelle Stewart, Ahmed Afzal, Bill Baskin, and Lisa Jean Moore all read portions of the book and offered their generous input. Special thanks go to Morris Kaplan and Rudolf Gaudio, who read the manuscript in its entirety during an especially busy time.

Scott Webel, friend and editor extraordinaire, helped me to polish the book, making suggestions that helped me improve my arguments and others that kept me thinking and inspired. I also thank the external reviewers who helped me to strengthen my claims and who even appreciated its "mundane" voice. Beth Bouloukos and Laurie Searl at SUNY Press offered the book a home and helped it to see print. My friend Rory Golden provided the gorgeous cover art.

Although this book draws only a little on my research on sex publics in Austin, Texas, the thinking that shaped that project and my subsequent work benefited from a brilliant and politically attuned graduate cadre, including, in no particular order, Junaid Rana, Peggy Brunache, Ken Rubin, Jennifer Goett, Jacqueline Polvora, Celeste Henery, Teresa Velasquez, Lynn Selby, Mathangi Krishnamurthy, Diya Mehra, Nicholas Copeland, Whitney Battle, and many others. I was also fortunate to benefit from the institutional and financial support of the Austin School of Diaspora Studies and the Center for African and African American Studies. Edmund Gordon, João Costa Vargas, Jafari Sinclaire Allen, Charlie Hale, Sharon Bridgforth, and Joni Jones/Omi Osun helped to shape

a vibrant intellectual and political culture, and they played an important role in shaping a generation of black scholars. Charlie Hale, Kamala
Visweswaran, and John Hartigan each demonstrated, albeit very differently, ways of bringing academic and political cultures together.

My conception of an academic life, and how to make it livable, was
shaped by many exceptional mentors, including Katya Gibel Mevorach,
Begoña Aretxaga (missed by many), and Dána-Ain Davis. Neville Hoad
and Katie Stewart deserve special thanks for their ongoing support and
friendship. Katie Stewart taught me how to cultivate the pleasures of
an ordinary life, and I continue to find her writing and lateral thinking
enormously inspiring. More recently, I have, like many others before me,
benefited from the kind wisdom of Henry Abelove, mensch and gentle-
man. I also thank Lauren Berlant, whose theorizations of intimacy made
this book possible. She models an engaged scholarship that addresses the
pressing political, aesthetic, and moral issues of our times with brilliance,
force, no small measure of humor, and an abiding commitment to the
power of pedagogy.

I also wish to thank the men (and some women) who shared their
stories with me. In the face of anxieties about creeping homonormativity, they have all impressed upon me the vitality of queer cultures. Finally,
I express my gratitude to those who helped me broaden and nurture my
understanding of intimacy in very material ways, who fruitfully disrupted my fantasies of self-sovereignty, who disorganized me and held me ac-
countable, who taught me about attachment, losing, and learning to love
more gracefully. Jasper White, Jason Brown, and Thomas Beard moved
me with their creativity and passion. Daniel Alexander Jones shared his
fierce liveness and taught me about the necessity of communion. This
book is dedicated to Amit Menachem Gilutz: to the immanence of intimacy.

Introduction

> A life contains only virtuals. It is made up of virtualities, events, singularities. What we call virtual is not something that lacks reality but something that is engaged in a process of actualization following the plane that gives it its particular reality. The immanent event is actualized in a state of things and of the lived that make it happen.
>
> —Gilles Deleuze, "Immanence: A Life"[1]

This book is about what it feels like to connect, or fail to, in a technophilic and technophobic present in which intimacy has gone virtual, if it ever was real. We depend on communications technologies to facilitate our lives and our interactions with others; we look to new media for succor from our loneliness, to bring us into contact with others we might love, hate, or remain stubbornly indifferent to. The virtual operates as a promise of immanence, the indwelling force of things waiting, pressing, ready to act. As an immanent power, the virtual is often deferred, sometimes materialized, but always charged with the *capacity* to help us feel like we belong. Intimacy describes: a *feeling* of connection or a *sense* of belonging; embodied and carnal sensuality, that is, *sex*; and that which is *most inward or inmost* to one's personhood. Intimacy is also a vast assemblage of ideologies, institutional sites, and diverse sets of material and semiotic practices that exert normative pressures on large and small bodies, lives, and worlds. In contemporary U.S. culture, intimacy names the affective encounters with others that often matter most, while also functioning as a juridical form, an aspirational narrative, and therapeutic culture's raison d'être.[2] All of this is to say that intimacy refers to things we feel and do, and it is a force.

Intimacy has been a central site in the culture wars of the last thirty years. According to many among the political Right, intimacy's well-being, even its essential nature, has suffered under the onslaught of multiculturalism and other minority demands for inclusion. This perceived war has led to entrenched, if wholly irrational, positions, especially among the Right: to take only one example, miscegenation may no longer be a focal point of anxiety, at least not in polite company, but gay marriage operates in its stead as a new scapegoat for the failures, real and imagined, suffered by heterosexual marriage and the family and nation writ large.[3] New technologies have added fuel to these anxious fires. Utopian cyberspace discourses, whose optimism is now viewed with both disdain and nostalgia, were always tempered by technophobic panics that turned on questions of intimacy, especially of the more carnal sort. Cyberspace promised infinite pleasures and freedoms, especially freedoms from the constraints of gender and sex—if your wife wouldn't do it you could find someone, even a bot, who'd do it for you online, without making you take out the trash—and at the same time evoked and reproduced fears about those kinds of sex that stepped outside the bounds of what anthropologist Gayle Rubin famously called "the charmed circle" of socially sanctioned sexuality.[4] The Web, or so the fears went, would usher in an anarchic wave of sexual libertinism. And in a way, these fears were true. New digital media technologies, including but not limited to the Internet, have facilitated a new era of casual or anonymous hookups (Craigslist), CGI safe sex alternatives and role playing (Second Life), and, of course, the proliferation of masturbatory aids (DIY porn).

But these new freedoms and possibilities picked up anxieties like Velcro.[5] Virtual intimacies signaled new possibilities even as they foregrounded the perceived failures of intimate belonging. Virtual intimacies were failures before the fact. If you had to get online to get it, it couldn't be the real thing. But what is the real thing, what is real intimacy?

Virtual Intimacies laterally answers this question by focusing on the experiences of gay men, including myself, who have navigated this expansive and expanding field of virtually mediated intimacies, who go on the hunt for love or sex and who often find themselves entangled—in the love and sex they were seeking or in other, less predictable encounters—along the way. Rather than a smooth space that flows,[6] digital virtuality amplifies the inconstant stutter of desire. The technologies we hope will facilitate connection can instead block or confuse it. We might not have access to technology or have the literacy to use it. New digital divides are constituted not only by who has access to the Internet but by the specific points of access—blacks and Latinos, for example, increasingly use proprietary mobile phones to access the Web—and bandwidth. Sometimes things get messy when we can't get something to work, it doesn't work the way we want, or our lack of knowledge or foreknowledge means we screw things up (like leaving our Facebook profile public, or posting a face pic on a Craigslist personal ad, or accidentally cc-ing someone on an e-mail they weren't meant to have and not knowing how to recall it). Then there are standbys such as sexual shame (and its respectable effect, sexual propriety) that forty years after Stonewall doggedly cling to queer sex, materializing in persistent social stigma about sexual practices ("I'm okay with gays as long as they don't *flaunt* it") and the everyday bullying overheard in schools around the country ("hey, faggot"). The fluidity and playfulness of cyberspace and the intimate possibilities it was supposed to afford have been punctured by corporeality; for me and some of my informants, for example, the particularities of our racial enfleshments have operated as obvious and not so obvious drags on our erotic or romantic possibilities.[7]

I began researching this book during the dotcom boom and bust in Austin, Texas, at the turn of the last millennium. I wanted to know what the Internet offered queerness and vice versa—how it might shape or be shaped by its encounter with queer ideas and bodies. What I found was that while I could apply some of the excited rhetoric about cyberspace to what it felt like to be online—sex was easy to get, people could come out without fearing for their well-being, people could explore and experiment with their identities and the sorts of sex they wished they were having—the truth was much messier and less optimistic. You might be able to get dick to your house faster than a pizza, as one early informant told me, but for many the dick might be late, it might ask for an exorbitant tip, or it might not be hot anymore when it did arrive. By the early aughts, the exciting newness of this virtual medium—as in the chat rooms at Gay.com or in gay IRC—had morphed into something altogether more banal. People still complained about the sex they had or couldn't get; they still got the clap; and they engaged in binge/purge cycles, meeting guys for early morning one-offs, then swearing off Netsex forever.

Increasingly, I encountered narratives of loss and addiction, anomie and nostalgia for the days before the Net. My research came to focus less on these new technologies than on the time and spaces that preceded them, on the intimate worlds formed around practices of cruising parks and toilets, and around the many losses, material and affective, suffered from AIDS. These losses were contagious, creating an affective atmosphere that implicated and troubled me. I was relatively new to my gay tribe, and I experienced more than a little culture shock. My critique—of the neoliberal impact of gentrification on public sex and on the ways virtual spaces supplemented without supplanting sex in public toilets—was contaminated,[8] and my epistemic certainties undone. The queer worlds I had hoped to find were a little too "brave new" for my liking, and they were saturated with melancholia and nostalgia. But they also turned me on and tuned me in—I learned that sex was a kind of background hum, that every space might become a queer space, if only I paid attention to sometimes faint but almost always present erotic frequencies: gazes held a second too long, subtle and not so subtle movements and gestures (a casual grope or a hand resting near a crotch), alert lingering in gym showers and saunas, or the peculiarly intense studying that goes on near some university toilets, especially out of the way ones.

Queer spaces, I learned, were spaces where normal rules of social intercourse were suspended, especially those defined by heteronormative ideals that permitted homosociality but discouraged homosex and emphasized sexual propriety. They were also spaces whose properties were creatively reworked to accommodate sexual pleasures—bathrooms became sites for impromptu late afternoon collective jerk off sessions, and after the bars closed, parks became landscapes of whispered conversations and half-seen figures. None of this is to say that these spaces were uniquely liberatory (there were still the closet, crabs, and the cops to think about), but they did come to represent for me something of the expansiveness of queer sexual practices that I had thought lost with HIV/AIDS and growing mainstream acceptance.

After leaving Austin, my home and fieldsite for seven years, I returned to the digitally mediated sites and events that first caught my ethnographic attention. This book collects a few of those reflections.

These now not so new virtual intimacies encounter and rework historical antecedents particular to queer, especially gay male, sociality: chiefly cruising and hooking up. These forms of contact and encounter have been famously celebrated by black gay science fiction writer and critic Samuel R. Delany, who writes elegiacally of New York public sex venues; for him these spaces of public sex afforded rare opportunities for "interclass contact and communication conducted in a mode of good will."[9] While a handful of other texts have emerged over the last decade that treat cruising and casual sex as important to histories of gay social formation, modestly recuperating promiscuous or libertine practices,[10] they are largely relegated to an earlier, almost primitive, period of sexual practice. Neoliberal ideologies and the moralism of the New Right together effectively curtailed a collective politics of sexual liberation. The successes of these views are apparent in the ways many gays view public sex as antiquated, dangerous, and disgusting. And though new media affords the possibility of cruising, this is limited to the context of personal choices and consumerist self-styling. Hookup sites and cruising apps reduce social worlds of public sex to bad faith erotic free markets; they are in bad faith because like the neoliberal economies in which they are situated, the benefits of the market tend to accrete to the very few—namely, well to do, young, and very often white, men. New media also paradoxically literalize widely circulating views about their historical antecedents: such intimacies are *merely* virtual.

Transitory and often anonymous, these intimacies were nonetheless vital in the formation of queer social networks well before the advent of specifically digital communications technologies. The queer network has a longer history. There were the networks produced through word of mouth, through spaces of contact and encounter (such as bars or zones tied to cruising), through medical and educational tracts, through jurisprudence, and through earlier communication media. Historian Martin Meeker explicitly links modern gay identity formation to these media, arguing that the consolidation of gay and lesbian communities depended on the ways people "could connect to knowledge about homosexuality."[11] Before gays could "come out," they had to be "'connected to' the knowledge that same-sex attraction meant something, that it had social ramifications, and that it had a name."[12] Meeker identifies three major trends in queer communication networks between the 1930s and 1970s: the formation of authoritative and candid networks (by gays themselves and not just by medical, legal, or educational discourses); mass mediated images that featured the "discovery" of homosexual networks; and DIY, commercial, and activist media that paralleled and contributed to strong subcultural formations in late 60s and the 1970s.[13]

These earlier analog networks, like the digital ones that preoccupy me, reflect what Alexander Galloway highlights as dominant tropes of the network: as web of ruin and chain of triumph. A net is a device of capture and work, "an act of doing and the structure or thing resulting from the act."[14] Networks are systems of "interconnectivity" in which parts are in constant relation, and they are "symbols for, or actual embodiments of, real world power and control."[15] As a web of ruin or a chain of triumph, networks tend to produce or reflect order or disorder. This conceptualization is useful in part for the ways it helps me to understand some of the perspectives of my earliest interlocutors who, in telling me stories about the halcyon days of gay sex in the 1970s, attributed the waning of that period not so much to AIDS but to the very successes of the gay rights movement. By bringing sexuality to the fore, the movement effectively created sexuality as a kind of identitarian demand—everyone had to have a sexuality, and gays needed to be out of the closet. Rather than loose affective, experiential, or affinal ties, identity politics demanded stickier sorts of belonging, favoring identities and communities over impersonal socialities or a commons where they might encounter one another. My informants recollected earlier erotic socialities, non-identitarian collectivities and scenes of contact, impersonal events and singularities of lives lived in and through differently textured experiences and relations, not, or not only, in and through frozen categories of identity. Thus, the (however modest) achievements of gay lobbying efforts—a chain of triumph, in Galloway's terms—created order in a messy and capacious world of public sexual encounters, limiting rather than expanding emotional and erotic opportunities (among others). Internet-based cruising and hookup sites likewise represented both chain of triumph and web of ruin among my informants. For many young gay men interested in expanding their social and erotic associations, IRC, chat rooms, and the like helped them to bypass bars or public sex spaces or the sometimes lengthy process of introduction that occurs through face-to-face social networking. They could get online and find exactly what they were looking for when they wanted it. But many older gay men despaired at these new digital spaces and not necessarily because they found them difficult to use. Rather, they perceived online spaces as ruinous because of the ways they foreclosed the possibility of the random encounter, or the unpredictable bloom of desire. They reasoned, and rightly so, that if people entered in the qualities they thought they wanted in a search engine, they would be less open to other possibilities that might occur in real world queer spaces. The arguments I make here likewise explore the Janus-like effects of networks on intimate encounters.

On a very basic level, *Virtual Intimacies* describes a range of contacts and encounters, from the ephemeral to the enduring, made possible by digital and networked means: chat rooms, instant messaging, porn, status updates, tweets, online personals, dating sites, hookup apps, sexts.

Virtual Intimacies also captures a dominant cultural attitude about these phenomena: they're trouble, a diminished and dangerous corruption of the real thing. These beliefs have been widely refracted in and through mainstream media. A famous *Time* magazine cover from 1995, for example, features the morphed image of a child at a keyboard, whose shocked expression is eerily lit by a computer screen. The headline: "CYBERPORN EXCLUSIVE: A new study shows how pervasive and wild it really is. Can we protect our kids—and Free Speech?" While the debates about children's sexuality are a structuring element of debates about the Internet (see chapter 4), anxious fantasies about the impact of new communication media on intimacy were and remain widespread, variously fixating on the ways porn consumption negatively impacts desire (even turning some otherwise straight men's desires queer),[16] the ways virtual affairs via webcams or virtual worlds threaten marriages (or more rarely, lead to them), or on the hours whiled away to gaming (the stereotypical basement dwelling nerd). Digital media, and especially the Web, ushered in a new wave of technology-based disorders that, according to some, produced antisocial, anti-intimate behavior. In this context, addiction operates as an always at hand analytic to explain the lure and danger of virtual worlds, though these arguments confuse whether it's addiction or the pleasures of the Web that are cause or effect.

Most of the stories in this book refract these dominant cultural beliefs that virtual intimacies are failed intimacies that disrupt the flow of a good life lived right, that is, a life that involves coupling and kids, or at least, coupling and consumption. From this critical point of view, virtual intimacies approach normative ideals about intimacy but can never arrive at them; they might index some forms of connection or belonging, but not the ones that really count; they are fantastic or simulated, imaginative, incorporeal, unreal. Such characterizations resemble dominant beliefs about queer intimacies as pale imitations or ugly corruptions of the real deal—monogamously partnered, procreative, married, straight intimacy. Each of the chapters in the book highlights these widely circulating notions, foregrounding some of the ways queer belonging, mediated intimacies, and failure orbit one another in the popular imaginary.

But there's room yet for optimism. Thus, I do not simply, or not only, point to the fallacy or injustice of such attitudes. Rather, working from Deleuzean conceptions of the virtual, I offer two arguments that run laterally to the normative ones above. First, I underscore the ways virtuality is not opposed to the real; virtuality refers to immanence, capacity, and potentiality. Second, I underscore the ways intimacy is already virtual in the ways it is made manifest through affective experience.

For Gilles Deleuze the virtual refers to an immanent plane of potential, to the capacities something is capable of. "A life," Deleuze says, "contains only virtuals. . . . What we call virtual is not something that lacks reality but something that is engaged in a process of actualization following the plane that gives it its particular reality."[17] The virtual is something waiting or pressing, something sensed, something dreamed or remembered.[18] It is that which is so in essence, but not actually so. It is real but not concrete, ideal but not abstract.[19] It is a vitality not fully captured by form.

In *The Virtual,* anthropologist Rob Shields usefully outlines a range of historical virtualities, from the Reformation's insistence that the Eucharist was virtually rather than actually real, the illusionistic simulations of *trompe l'oeil* in Baroque painting and architecture, to the panoramas of the nineteenth century that sought to provide a total view of a scene or event. Shields also looks to rituals and rites of passage as "liminoid virtualities." In these practices and spaces, ordinary life is suspended and another reality takes precedence, a reality that, echoing Deleuze and Guattari's fascination with "becomings," empowers a transformation from one state of being to another.

As scholars of sexuality before and since Foucault have observed, queers have been especially adept at transforming intimate worlds and forms of sociality.[20] Virtuality helps to name the incipient social and affective worlds—modes of encounter, material configurations, emotional possibilities—that queer publics create, nourish, and sustain. Queers have made artful lives, and we have generated new affective dispositions. Affection, as the capacity to affect or be affected, is likewise virtual.[21] In this book I am preoccupied with affective states such as anxiety and optimism that are produced in and through virtual relationalities and mediated intimacies. Intimacy is not itself a form of affect; rather it is more like affect's own immanence—proximity, connection—a necessary precondition for certain affective states to bloom, especially those that have to do with other people. Affect happens in and through intimacy.

Intimacy is supported by a range of discourses and practices, but as an experience it is composed largely of feelings, feeling more or less connected, as if one belongs or doesn't. In this way, intimacy is and always has been virtual. As an assemblage of power relations, intimacy is scripted, even if those scripts are diverse and sometimes contradictory, but this does not mean there is no room for maneuver, for minor or major interventions in the ways extant intimacies might be reworked or new ones cultivated. That is, virtuality is one way to conceptualize intimacy's own ongoing immanence. Getting online is one way to understand this, but not the only one.[22]

I therefore do two things in this book: First, I track some of the ways technologically mediated intimacies are framed in popular, mass-mediated discourses as failed, establishing an equivalence between virtuality, failure, and queerness. In stories about public or online sex, sexual predators, or porn, anxieties about virtually mediated intimacy are also stories about the failure of queer desire and sex. However, describing the virtual as a failure to be intimate also exposes the fault lines of intimacy writ large. Thus, secondly, each of the chapters that follow also turns this framing of virtual intimacies as failed on its head, asking, What's real about intimacy to begin with? I do this not, or not only, to cynically challenge the intimacies people experience or more or less enjoy, but to recuperate the expansive possibilities that inhere in the notion of virtuality as immanence, as potential. The messy material encounters that come with sex show among other things, for example, the ways carnality can function as a creative political, even pedagogical, practice that resists and elaborates dominant narratives of intimacy. In this way, I work to show how virtual intimacies, rather than signaling the failure or corruption of intimate belonging, underscore the ways intimacy still possesses unrealized capacities and lines of flight.

At first blush, these arguments might seem too local or naively utopian. Do the ways same-sex desiring men desire one another or use technology to connect matter in a global context of environmental degradation, brutal repression, and imperialism? Do they matter to the apparent victory of neoliberal capitalism, or are they even perhaps symptomatic of its success? After all, isn't the promise of the virtual like the promise of the market, an unattainable thing we long for, the very longing for which does us harm?[23] While I understand virtual intimacies as situated within the circuits of what Jodi Dean calls "communicative capitalism,"[24] the commodified self-styling and interactive exchanges that express the democratic freedom to produce the self but only in and through fantasies of the market, there is also, I suggest, an uncaptured immanence and excess: the typically invisible but nonetheless present alternatives to the hegemonic forces that demand we believe that There is No Alternative to neoliberal hegemony.

Ideologies and institutions of intimacy under neoliberalism have increasingly incorporated and absorbed otherwise oppositional energies, domesticating the subcultural styles and resistant practices particular to queerness. Homonormativity, only recently a tantalizing theoretical possibility that described nascent homo incorporations into the mainstream, has crystallized into a matter of fact.[25] And while queer theory has never managed to become institutionally ensconced, queerness as a kind of quasi-awry thread in the multicultural fabric of U.S. mass culture has become a more permanent fixture: we've had New Queer Cinema, *Queer Eye,* Ellen, *The L Word,* Lady Gaga, and an ever-expanding array of gay supporting characters (we make great best friends). Since 9/11, homonormativity has also taken new forms, participating as homonationalism in a larger assemblage of state policies and discourses that buttress the permanent states of political emergency and exception that in turn work, increasingly desperately, to secure U.S. economic and cultural hegemony around the world.[26] Gay "freedoms" are metonymically linked to the freedoms of democracy and the market, and they are used to obscure the rapaciousness of imperialist and corporate hegemonies.[27]

Virtual intimacies, as immanent and expanding possibilities, might appear to mirror the logic of normative and nationalist structures of power (of both the hetero and homo varieties) that promise endless freedom and choice. But insofar as they congeal failed, carnal, ambivalent, and over- or hypermediated forms of intimate encounter (public sex, online hookups, predation, and so on), they also reflect the most irredeemable of queer intimacies, intimacies unlikely to be trumpeted as desirable freedoms. In this way, virtual intimacies also resist incorporation into the unreflective, deeply cynical, and/or phantasmatic celebrations of freedom that support homonational and neoliberal ideologies. Again, part of what I am trying to recuperate—intimacy's virtuality or immanence—is about trying to imagine forms of connection and belonging that are not necessarily identitarian and that do not fit neatly into our beliefs about how we might belong to a couple, a family, or nation. I labor to render intimacy as a "structure of feeling," as social and psychic, as an entangled contact zone of political and personal energies,[28] as constrained by *and* outside an overdetermined politics of identity, sexual or otherwise. Of course, the attendant dangers of this perspective are outlined by the critiques of homonormativity and homonationalism. By favoring experience as a more vital phenomenological engagement with the world over identity as a preformed and socially scripted category, I risk reproducing a depoliticized and narcissistic individualism: "experience," after all, and its seemingly endless permutation as such is precisely what is at stake and for sale in communicative capitalism and in the triumphalist networks of online commerce. But part of the promise of my approach (to the immanent and the open) is that it underscores the constructionist maxim that personhood is not necessarily constituted by what one does, but by how one feels, and by the ways one names those feelings (or doesn't) and puts them into relationship (or doesn't) with larger social histories of difference or national belonging. (Men who have sex with men aren't always gay, nor should they have to be. Queerness might refer to an oppositional political movement, or the refusal to be named as such.) Intimate virtuality in this way communicates fragile, ambivalent, but nonetheless real, experiential, and ethical movements that strain against (without fully escaping) the limits of identitarian forms. Intimacy builds worlds, affective, social, institutional, and otherwise; framing intimacy as virtual and as queer, rather than distorting or diminishing intimacy's "reality," defiantly argues for its expansion.

The book is divided into five chapters. Each tells a story about virtual intimacy and cuts across a range of mediated sites and spaces: the policing of public sex in Austin, Texas, juxtaposed with sex scandals suffered by conservative ideologues; the cultivation of new forms of intimacy in the popular online game *The World of Warcraft*; the emotional challenges black gay men face while navigating online gay sex publics; the ways the collectively imagined "erotic innocence" of children is mobilized to police sex in the digital age; and the creative transformation of "porn into life" by new queer DIY pornographers. In each chapter, I explore the ways some mediated form of connection, typically erotic, is perceived to have gone awry: the licentiousness of the Net gives way to predation (chapters 1 and 4), online games transform intimacy into a means to an end (chapter 2), online racisms produce all too affective dis-ease (chapter 3), and shared DIY porn emerges as antiporn activism's exemplar of internalized misogyny and false consciousness (chapter 5). Taken together, these chapters offer a snapshot, admittedly partial, of our virtually intimate present in which some forms of sex, like those in public or online, become the castigated and fascinating objects of mass culture, while simultaneously representing the birth of new forms of sociality.

The tensions in the titular idea—the ideological or affective entanglements that stick to and emerge from the collision of the virtual and intimate—are expressed through the interplay of a handful of themes, namely failure, anxiety, scandal, and loss, as well as creativity, play, and optimism. These themes come to life through stories men told me or that I, more or less confessionally, reveal to the reader. In each chapter, then, I attend to the regulatory efforts to glom desire onto normative ready-made paths, to harness and distribute its potential toward "good" objects and ends such as "real" or steady forms of attachment, while also emphasizing the labors, perverse and otherwise, that animatedly rework categories of intimacy in more novel and compelling ways.

Chapter 1, "The Virtual Life of Sex in Public," elaborates virtual intimacy's relation to talk about and feelings of failure. It brings together stories about sex in Austin, Texas, a city famous both for its high-tech aspirations and, among gay men, a lively cruising culture, with recent mass-mediated sex scandals and an appearance on the voyeuristic TV show about Internet predation, *To Catch a Predator*. I outline how talk about "sex in public," which includes actual public sex acts and mass-mediated panics about sex, reproduces a hierarchy of erotic value in which some forms of sex are more or less real than others. At the same time, I emphasize the ambivalence of this hierarchy: the mass public (that means us) takes pleasure in others' sexual failures while also uncomfortably recognizing the ways failures of all sorts nestle, even if only virtually, within our own intimacies. The fears and pleasures associated with failure structure what counts as intimate sociality and operate to police the possible forms intimacy might take; they are the none-too-subtle reminders about what's inside and what's outside ideal relational forms (the couple, the family, the nation).

In chapter 2, I look to the intimacies afforded by and creatively retooled within the hugely successful, massively multiplayer online game *The World of Warcraft*. "Intimacies in the Multi(player)verse" narrates my own entry into this game world that, with more than eleven million players from around the world, is the most successful game of its kind. Shadowing its success, however, are stories about addiction, alienation, breakups, and even death from overplay. However, I argue that intimacy, rather than extinguished by the game, is actually central to the experience of play. The game design in fact effectively requires that players play with one another to succeed; intimacy becomes transactional and instrumental, a necessary means to an end. I show how players interrupt this demand to be intimate in particular ways by using in-game chat channels to have virtual sex, transforming intimate sociality into a means *without* an end.

"Feeling Black and Blue" asks, What does it feel like to be black and queer in online gay sex publics? The answer: more than a little sore. Here, I detail my own experiences and those of other black gay men who have used online gay spaces for love and sex. Chapter 3 is organized around three dominant feelings: anxiety, paranoia, and optimism. Anxiety is a heightened, speculative form of attention, in this case, to the incomplete knowledge of how race might matter in virtual contexts. Paranoia extends racial anxiety into a more certain world in which race decidedly does matter, but only in the worst sorts of ways, as stereotype and cruel rejection. Finally, in my discussions of optimism, I try to recover something of the virtual's openness, emphasizing the possibilities that, even in the face of racism or the failure to connect, still inhere in these online publics.

Chapter 4, "Justin Fucks the Future," tells the story of Justin Berry, former underage "camwhore" turned anti–sex predator tech consultant. This chapter rehearses Berry's narrative of abuse (his online performances for older men), underage sexual ambivalence (although he had sex with boys and girls, he really got online to meet girls his own age), and dangerous (because he was immature) tech entrepreneurism. This narrative was told and retold on the pages of *The New York Times,* Oprah, and CNN. My rehearsal of this story serves more queer purposes: I challenge Berry's tale of innocence lost and redemption gained. I point to the tacit homophobia in media representations of his story and the ways in which anxieties about childhood sexuality are tied to fears of technological change to show the ways the figure of the Child, a virtual exemplar of moral purity and risk, fixes the limits of erotic possibility. Reading mainstream reports against the grain, drawing on counternarratives and legal documents, I suggest that Justin Berry's abuse is altogether more complex than it appears at first glance and that his story is equally about public fascination with underage sex and overblown fears about technologically sophisticated gay predators.

Turning from the more critical tone of the last chapter, chapter 5, "The *Élan Vital* of DIY Porn," gestures toward a more generous and open reading of intimate virtuality. In it, I playfully employ philosopher Henri Bergson's notion *élan vital,* or vital force, to describe new online gay DIY porn. Situating these contributions to our collective, and increasingly digital, pornographic imagination within a larger history of gay porn, I suggest that DIY porn importantly challenges some of the organizing principles of commercial or industrial porn. I point to the ways DIY porn frequently operates in gift rather than market economies, cultivates the participation of ordinary people (as performers and as fans), interrupts the aesthetic banality of mainstream pornographic texts, and situates itself within explicitly political, pro-sex, feminist, and queer frameworks. In this way, porn, rather than functioning only as dead or deadening representations of sex, operates as a creative and enlivening practice of life in the twenty-first century.

This is a book that has since its inception risked being out of time, at arriving too late or missing the contemporaneity of its objects. The acceleration of media forms and the (often enviable) speed with which (largely nonacademic) commentators express their views on them means that the new media that shape the virtual intimacies I am preoccupied with have always risked becoming old media. But queer temporalities are extensive, attached to lengthy (sometimes lifelong) adolescences, to ephemeral presents, and to futures that often sidestep the promises and linearity of straight time, like the punctums of marriage and kids.[29] The ethnographic research that shaped this book took place online over the last ten years, but in that time, the digital landscape changed dramatically. Where IRC and other chatrooms were once the primary sites for interactive exchange, the boom of Web 2.0, in which user-generated content has played an increasingly important role, as well as new social media platforms such as Facebook and Twitter, have made interactivity central to the digital everyday. As Henry Jenkins and others point out, contemporary media ecologies are characterized by "convergence," a central element of which includes the ways consumers become producers of content.[30] And while this book certainly attends to user-driven content and the technologies that enable them, technologies themselves are not its focus, but rather, the kinds of discourses in which technologies are situated and the contacts they afford.

Finally, a brief note on this book's tone: I have sometimes been accused of not "sounding academic," a phrase that arrives as a criticism when followed by the word "enough" and as a compliment when it arrives from my students. I have written this book with students, my own and others', in mind, while also trying to maintain the intellectual rigor of the concepts that I engage. I perform what Melissa Gregg, analyzing the work of Meagan Morris, describes as "a mundane voice." This voice embodies a mode of critical engagement that draws on "anecdote, an affective tone, a colloquial focus" to humble cultural studies' projects while still cultivating forms of curiosity and interest "with the aim of rendering legible new political performances."[31] It is a way of enacting how experiences, including those of the researcher or analyst, are nested in larger social worlds—what Lauren Berlant calls "theorizing in living,"[32] thereby introducing complicating layers into the project of cultural analysis, and, I hope, minimizing the often unnecessary alienation produced by the use of jargon. And in its use of direct address, especially "you" and "we," I mark the ways the public of this book is already shaped by factors of education, class, and social location (you bought this book, or you got it from a library), but I also use these forms of address to invite readers' participation in the publics the book charts, publics readers might otherwise find alien or unfamiliar. By hailing readers in this way, I aim for the text to shrink the distance between the worlds the book describes and the one the reader finds herself in.

In this way, I hope for the book itself to function as an intimate gesture, one that through its attention to feelings and the worlds feelings build draws its readers close, encouraging them to reflect on the sorts of intimacies we have lived (and mourned or celebrated), and to the ones that tease the edge of our imagination, that stretch what we think is doable and ethical in our encounters with ourselves or others. This is not only to say that we need more or better, deeper or meaningful intimacies, or that this book presents any actionable self-help solutions to the problems that inevitably seem to attend our intimacies. Indeed, in its emphasis on the immanence of the virtual, it follows both the most normative beliefs in intimacy—especially the idea that intimacy, in the form of true love or a nourishing attachment is waiting, just around the corner—and their inverse—you don't have to be close to feel connected or feel close to be connected. However, my emphasis on virtuality also serves less ambiguously as a reminder that intimacy is possessed of an inherent and generative capacity for change.

CHAPTER ONE

The Virtual Life of Sex in Public

In this chapter, I examine various scenes of intimacy's failure, juxtaposing recent mass mediated sex scandals with ethnographic research I conducted in Austin, Texas, a city famous both for its high technology aspirations and for its cruising culture. I speculate on the ways various discourses on sex in public and virtually mediated eroticism try to capture and frame different iterations of "sex in public" as failures: the inability to achieve idealized forms of erotic belonging is variously expressed as expectancy, deferral, lack, and as an inability to arrive, achieve, or actualize normative forms of belonging.

Located in both specific places and larger circuits of public culture, the chapter tracks the ways the practices and discourses that congeal around sex in public position it as a form of virtual intimacy, that is, as a diminished or pathological form of contact whether it happens between two people or many. Whether practiced by communities of men in Austin, Texas, by putatively straight Republican senators, or by the American "Everyman" of Dateline's *To Catch a Predator,* the erotic or affective acts that jump into public consciousness as perversion, scandal, hypocrisy, and predation operate as both the limit of and the ground for normative models of relationality. That is, in these often-spectacular public failures, the architecture and trajectory of heteronormative aspirations—the chase after and promise of a life realized in the image of the monogamous couple—are arrested and interrupted by those aspirations' queer excesses. At the same time, these failures operate to police the possible forms intimacy might take; they

[handwritten marginalia: queerness AS excess]

17

are none-too-subtle reminders about what's inside and what's outside ideal relational forms (the couple, the family, the nation).

In much of what follows, the ways in which sex in public is so persistently diminished works in parallel with the profound sense of pleasure that is taken in witnessing the failure of other people's intimate lives, especially when these failures are tied to virtual or online spaces. Our fascination with these various scenes and scandals is thus also perhaps tied to the fascination we have for a failure that is more fundamentally constitutive of intimacy itself. Insofar as intimacy defers or delays concrete epistemological certainty (does he *really* love me? what about in ten years?), it fails to actualize the fantasy, aspiration, or dream that makes it vital. This is true even for those forms of intimacy, including concrete forms of sexual practice, that appear undeniably real. Sex, as any good slut will tell you, doesn't have to be connected.

Indeed, the only surety here is that failure and liveness are in some sort of relation, and the near certainty of failure is part of the vitality, too. But we also watch for the promise of the norm's transgression (as Bataille puts it, "In the transgression of the prohibition, a spell is cast")[1] and the promise that there's something beyond transgression itself—not just sexual or relational utopias, but things we haven't even thought of yet. Within the larger framework that looks askew at most forms of sex in public as deeply flawed, or at intimacy itself as something that reproduces the possible but never the certain, there is then still a seed of hopefulness that might rescue sex in public or intimacy from cynicism or anti-relationality. This leads to a kind of foundational, and paradoxical, claim, namely, that from the perspective of the mass public, the virtualization of sex is seen at once as evidence of intimacy's degeneration while also keeping alive the hope for sexual possibility and difference. Virtualization is, on the one hand, tied to online or digital culture; on the other, it has to do with forms of sex that are deemed nonnormative or failed, sex in public key among them. Yet the disavowals of these forms of sex are also evocations that open up the possibility of difference, of things other than the norm. Although they are stigmatized, and in the case of same-sex sex in public doubly stigmatized (queer and public), they are nonetheless offered as one among other possible avenues for erotic fulfillment. And, regardless, even as particular acts are imbued with positive or negative values, the force of intimacy's potential keeps us coming back for more.

DISAVOWING SEX IN PUBLIC

Felix and I sat down in the chilly Japanese restaurant and ordered sake while we waited for Frederick to arrive. I'd met Fred before, and was eager to talk to him about my research on public sex. Felix promised me that Fred had some great cruising stories. Felix, of course, had his own stories, though we rarely talked in detail about what happened those nights I dropped him off near the gay bars to find hustlers, something that was easier to do in San Antonio than in Austin. In San Antonio, the cluster of gay bars near Main Street and McCullough, along with many of the adjacent streets, saw a lively traffic in drugs, hustling, and casual hookups. Perhaps because of its size or because it was generally considered to be a more conservative city, San Antonio's gay culture seemed especially alive—edgier, rougher, and more diverse. And while, by the mid to late 1990s, San Antonio's adult businesses had, like Austin's, also moved to the periphery of the city, the gentrification of its downtown has remained partial and incomplete. And though it is not a city known for its public parks like Austin, as a large and sprawling metropolitan area, cruisers had long put San Antonio parks to uses they had not been intended for, something I first learned about on a gay message board in early 1998.

When Frederick arrived, I was impressed, as usual, with how put together he looked. Mahogany skin, crisp dress shirt, shaved head, hip glasses. You'd never know he was sick. Even after his health really started to fail, he always seemed energetic, upbeat. And he was smart, too, finishing his PhD in psychology and already doing clinical work.

Frederick was in many ways a perfect object choice—an attractive, intelligent, professional black man. Yet he was also off limits. His "sickness"—the creeping power of the HIV virus—had already incapacitated him a few times. Thus, his current appearance belied something else, an incipient form of bodily breakdown against which my own desires crashed and went no farther. We never talked about it directly, about how this possible, probable failure of his body constrained his ability to actualize the vision of intimacy he'd articulated. The virus compounded the failure of intimacy; he failed to attract me. Eventually, too, he failed to live.

We ordered more sake and food, and we talked. I'd hoped Frederick would tell me stories about the public sex scene in San Antonio, to complement or complicate the more focused research I was conducting in Austin. At the same time, I was beginning to wonder whether stories about sex in public, along with the various attempts to manage and police it, didn't share qualities across different geographic spaces. In San Antonio, like Austin and most other large or even modestly sized cities, public sex was part of ordinary life and held an important place in many men's sexual histories, as did the efforts to police it. Public sex materialized in particular ways in specific locales; it was also an epiphenomenon critical to the formation of and ongoing coherence of same-sex erotic networks.

Frederick didn't disappoint:

> One day I'd gone running in Eisenhower Park in this cute little running outfit. I'd run along these trails and see who was out and about, get the lay of the land, you know. And once I'd gotten the better part of my run done, I'd slow down and loop back by the guys I thought were hot. A lot of these guys would be there on their lunch hours or on breaks. And since this was before they closed [some of] the military bases, there were a lot of soldiers and what not, too, though they weren't in uniform, you could still tell by their hair and how they held themselves. Sort of stiff, you know?
>
> This was a good day—I sucked off one guy in the bathroom and another in the bushes, and I was, you know, going to make another loop when I heard this noise, and I look up and there's this helicopter. Somehow, I get it in my head that it's there for me, so I start running. And I swear it follows me! I'm convinced they're coming for me, so I keep running until I thought I was going to die. I'd never been worried about it before, but after that I couldn't help but be paranoid.

Not long after, Fred learned he'd sero-converted, and after that it was a "public service to take myself out of commission." Narrating the excitement of the chase and the fear and grief that accompanied the knowledge that he'd become HIV positive, Fred's stories illustrated the differing meanings of "public" or publicness that emerges in the narratives of cruisers and others. There was the public of intimate strangers seeking contact in city parks; the public sometimes referred to, colloquially, as "the Man" that sought to police its own boundaries; and the public of friends and lovers that made up his larger queer social world that was at least in part a virtual public comprised of people he hadn't met or loved or fucked yet.

When I asked him, excepting pursuit helicopters, if he missed the sorts of intimacies public parks afforded him for so many years, he answered confidently, "not at all." In fact, to my surprise, he repudiated it. He said that while he didn't know whether he'd sero-converted because of public sex, he saw public sex as part of larger pattern of risk, irresponsibility, and above all else, a deeply troubled conception of and approach to intimacy. "It was fun," he admitted. "But it was wrong, too."

Though decidedly less ambivalent than some, Fred's repudiation of sex in public echoes other narratives, including those of Austinites I interviewed, and the conservative figures and the *TCAP* episode I discuss below. Indeed, very few people seemed eager to defend the intimacies that fall under the rubric of public sex. It sometimes seemed as if the refusal and rejection of sex in public had as much to do with a sense of hopelessness and impossibility, a sense that sex in public could never be "the real thing," as with anxieties about being outed or exposed to diseases. It was as if some force or congeries of them (the virus, capitalism, human nature, homophobia) had slammed shut the door to other possibilities and spaces of social and sexual belonging. At first glance, Fred's repudiation seemed tied to these beliefs, which while recognizing public sex as a common, indeed ordinary, part of life and the sexual histories of many, nonetheless framed it as an a priori failure of intimacy that deserved surveillance and punishment.

I pressed Fred. Well, if those forms of sexual intimacy that people experienced surreptitiously in public spaces were somehow insufficient or inadequate, what were the better alternatives? His response challenged me. Beginning from a *feeling* both affective and epistemological, he narrated both a deeply individual response and an ethical philosophy orientated to a larger social world.[2] "Almost definitely monogamous. *Closeness, sharing.* And I can be patient now." Fred made clear his model of intimacy was monogamous, but was this the same sort of monogamy demanded by heteronormativity? Was heteronormativity even an appropriate term for what Fred had so earnestly articulated? And to what degree was my reluctance to call it heteronormative affected by his illness and death, by my desire to do justice to his memory? At first glance, his apparently simple philosophy adhered to a normative script of intimacy, especially in the ways it articulated a vision of life, sex, and relating that begins from a place of wholeness rather than an often unconscious sense of inadequacy or lack. Yet, Fred hadn't simply appropriated wholesale tacit or mass-mediated conceptions of togetherness. Indeed, he rejected the notion that the couple form alone could be sufficient in satisfying his intimate needs. In this and other conversations held over the following year, he elaborated a web of relations, fragile, tenuous, and shot through with conflict as well as love. Explicitly drawing on black traditions of family, he imagined a partnership, extended kin networks, friendships, and gay social worlds as constituting something more vital. Intimacy wasn't something to be captured, but something to be experienced as the pressure, ephemerality, and multiplicity of desire.

Reflecting back on this conversation after many years, I realized that this is what Fred needed from relationality to live with himself and others, and more, to thrive. I am still challenged by this vision of belonging, a notion that itself deserves further, if brief, elaboration. In the context of an intimate partnership, belonging might have to do with the feeling or experience of mutual possession and recognition that gives one's identity and the relationship itself meaning. But in a larger social field, belonging is made of the affective or material ties and obligations that link the individual to others. While this second sense of relationships also encompasses a kind of ownership (for example, in the ways one belongs to a family, a community, or nation), I am most interested in the ways it produces or enforces feelings of closeness and distance. So what's challenging about this form of intimacy as belonging is that it involves pushing against the conception that one is self-sufficient. Instead, one answers to others and the explicitly and tacitly agreed upon conditions of the group. Feeling at home, one also has to keep house.

Fred hadn't simply accepted the notion that intimacy would succeed only in the monogamous couple form, or that his queerness needed to adhere to Andrew Sullivan's assimilationist and neoconservative articulation of the "virtually normal," in which the virtual refers to a kind of passing, an assimilationist "almost so."[3]

I admired and respected Fred, yet at the time I longed for the very sorts of encounters he described and disavowed. His response resonated in me as something constructed and true, honest and sentimental, traditional and revolutionary. After our first conversation, I studied some of the local gay message boards and listservs for clues about the park he had mentioned. Eventually, I spent the better part of a day trying to find Eisenhower Park, wandering through its dusty and largely empty trails without stumbling across a single person, not knowing what I might have done if I had. As in the collective queer memory that valorizes gay sex in the '60s and '70s, in the trucks and on the piers of New York, or in the ground floor bathrooms in the University of Texas Tower, I wanted to recuperate public sex as a grand, if largely disappeared, communal experiment. Someone I couldn't simply label and dismiss as conservative or an assimilationist contested my nostalgic and celebratory reconstruction of these intimate publics.

Even here, recounting this narrative, I am wary of the ways it seems to capture intimacy as something achievable given the right tool kit (self awareness, therapy, Oprah). What I am wary of, then, is the way this story seems to establish a concrete and positive content to the possibilities represented by "virtual intimacy," thereby offering a disappointing closure to what otherwise remains a more open and contested field of articulations and propositions. It's important, then, to point out that while Fred articulated an "answer" to the problem of virtual intimacy, that is, to the problem sex in public posed for him, this answer itself was in fact a deferral, a promise to himself and not an effect or a result. That is, on the most basic level, when his family and friends gathered to honor him and the webs of belonging he'd elaborated between them when he became very ill, there was no dutiful partner at his bedside. The success of his dream did not rest in the realization of the ideal couple form but in some other, tactible *and* ineffable form of relationality.

Closeness, sharing. Fred said this to Felix and me with the intensity of a revelation.

AUSTIN SEX PUBLICS

The stories men told me about public sex in Austin were varied, yet they shared a few common themes, even when they described very different orientations to sex in public, and increasingly, the role online spaces played in their lives. Whether men were for or against public sex, they frequently framed these practices in the context of one sort of failure or another.

In Austin, there was, throughout much of the 1980s and 1990s, a very active public sexual culture that centered around without being wholly dependent on university life. With many active tearooms, bathrooms used for public sex, the sprawling University of Texas complex and the adjacent "Drag" (Guadalupe Street between 21st and 32nd

Streets) attracted cruisers from around the country, as did the city's lush parks, a rarity in Texas. As a college town, and Texas' premiere liberal oasis, Austin was a central hub for the production of slackerdom and had, barring episodic crackdowns, a correspondingly lackadaisical sexual culture where, as it was put to me, "it was always easy to get laid." Steven Saylor, narrating his own relationship to Austin, says something similar, noting that even after AIDS had had a chilling effect on sex on the coasts, Austin was still rich with opportunities.[4]

During the period of my research, Austin still saw lively activity in its parks, though this waxed and waned with the interest of police and irritable residents, who sometimes complained they could see men cruising from their front porches. The University of Texas also contained an active sexual geography with a handful of sites—gyms and public bathrooms—that saw regular use. By 2002 and 2003 these had also attracted a regulatory gaze and the usually subtle attention of campus police and administrators whose efforts resulted in, among other things, glory holes being covered up and stall doors removed from especially active bathrooms (thus denying cruisers the modicum of privacy that public sex demands).

Yet even as stories about sex in Austin often highlighted the relative ease with which erotic encounters could be found across a range of urban and later online spaces, many if not most of the narratives were marked by loss and failure, whether characterized as nostalgia for disappeared places such as the porn theater on Congress Avenue, or the still painful wounds of losing friends and loved ones to AIDS. Some of my interlocutors told the stories of their erotic lives as tales of lost innocence: small town boy goes to the big city (even though Austin isn't that big) and falls into a world of drugs and herpes. And for some the sense of loss came later, after spaces like the Cinema West porn theater were shut down; or how, four years of therapy and three different kinds of antidepressants later, they were still alone.

The following brief ethnographic snapshots evoke a few of these narratives. The stories echo those of other men I spoke with in Austin and across the country as the visible political challenges to local and state varieties of homophobia increasingly dimmed and queer visibility became increasingly tied to the gentrification of neighborhoods and public debates about mainstreaming (marriage and military service). "Queering" gradually had less to do with a politicized attitude than with branded style.

Brad peppered many of his monologues on art, politics, and NPR with references to his dead partner, Terry. Terry was an artist, wild. If Brad took half a hit of acid, Terry would take three. Brad took care of Terry when he got sick and the illness was drawn out, melodramatic. A salon: over coffee and cigarettes in Brad's yard, our mutual friend Lynne and I would draw or paint while Brad spun one story after another, heartfelt if often unfinished polemics on politics, relationships, memories, and the dead. When our salon became difficult or awkward, as it increasingly did, it was because the world of the dead, a world to which Brad seemed inevitably drawn, a world of belonging and relationality marred by absences, unwilling or incomplete closures. Our own little world could not always bear the weight of the missing other.

Jasper fantasized about buying the chairs from Cinema West having heard they would be auctioned off after the police finally shut the porn theater and Austin institution down. When he first moved to town, he and his friends would hang out on South Congress near the theater. There were gay nights, too, but even when there weren't, queers gathered on the upper balcony. "I had a lot of good memories in those chairs." Yet the street traffic alarmed the nearby residents of Travis Heights, a then rapidly gentrifying neighborhood. And politicians likewise disliked the way the theater was a "blemish" on the avenue, the road that served as the gateway to the state capitol. Finally, in 1998, after years of intense pressure from city officials, police stings, harassment by moralists, speculation by real estate developers, and the efforts of some area residents, Cinema West was forced to close after twenty-one years of showing straight and gay pornographic films. Jasper never got his theater seat; turns out the sale was a rumor.

Shane lived alone, worked hard, and had stopped going out. But he showed me pictures of when he did, when he cruised Zilker Park, before he had to start going to funerals every week. These pictures showed a charismatic, smiling young man, arms draped around friends. Shane took me on a tour of Austin's disappeared queerspaces. We drove to the waterfront near the leather bar, the Chain Drive, to Pease Park, to Mount

Bonnell, and to Zilker. It was exciting to visit these spaces and to realize they held such erotically charged histories. Shane recounted stories about tricks, lovers, and fabulous parties. But by the end of our forays, we were tired and a little melancholy. Everywhere we'd gone had been empty.

Though "community" might bring together these different figures and their stories, "sex public" works just as well, especially given the central role sex plays in many of the men's narratives. Most of the men I spoke with about sex in Austin's public places described the way it was, for years, central to Austin's everyday queer geography.

Although there were many fond memories of encounters in public parks, bathrooms, or saunas at the university, very few were willing to defend those practices. Most of the men I spoke to situated sex in public in relation to some larger pathology, such as internalized homophobia or a fear of intimacy rather than describe it as a practice that brought men of different backgrounds together.

Public sex was also framed as part of a developmental narrative in which it had once been central to someone's sexual life but that, after getting in trouble or out of hand, or getting coupled, was abandoned in favor of other, less risky pursuits. And of course, many men shared the sense that public sex was something that only other, more abject people did. Finally, some felt as if even if there was nothing inherently wrong with public sex per se, the secrecy, shame, and risk of exposure transformed it into an altogether too dangerous endeavor. As in my discussion with Fred, very few of my interlocutors saw public sex as something to be celebrated or indeed as central to Austin's larger queer sex publics.

The ways in which online intimacies were embraced and disavowed echoed many of the stories about public sex that had been told to me. Gay men's contacts and encounters with one another were increasingly mediated by the queer space of the screen. And this increasingly ordinary mediation of belonging and sex through virtual means was met with no small amount of ambivalence.

I met Calico, like many of my informants, online. And though we talked intermittently for some time before we met in person, his story was fairly typical: life was better before its virtualization. When I met Calico for coffee to talk about virtual intimacies, he emphasized this point; he wanted to talk about that other gay life, the real one.

I was never online until a few years ago. I came to school here in 1981 back when gay life was really starting here from my perspective. Historically—I was here from 'eighty to 'eighty-seven and was out and in gay life—a lot of things influenced that lifestyle. Parallel things were happening as society was opening to gay life—like AIDS.

Gay life was much better then. You did things outside because the Internet wasn't around then, you didn't have that resource. You had to go to bars to find people. And they had much richer environments in terms of the diversity of people. But I didn't participate sexually because of the fear in the culture, I didn't know *where* or *how* people were getting it [AIDS].

Like so many others, Calico expressed his feelings about Austin's virtually mediated sex public in ambivalent terms. Yes, it was a means to connect, but other, older forms were better, even if they were fraught with risk. This is especially evident in Calico's story in which his nostalgia for a pre-Internet gay life is simultaneously marked by a failure to connect sexually. The emergence of ostensibly disembodied forms of communication engendered by online message boards, chat rooms, and so on retroactively enable a "a fantasy of bodily proximity or presence."[5] For Calico, life before the Web seems saturated by greater closeness, even if this did not translate into erotic encounters.

The virtual activates each of the above stories about sex and publicness, albeit in different ways. Austin's sex publics are both concrete and overlaid with a dense affective geography. That is, even actual spaces, such as parks and public bathrooms, are deeply tied to the past, to memories, and longing. And however ordinary these practices had been for the men I spoke with or for Austin's broader public culture, they were also implicitly and explicitly positioned as outside of other, more staid forms of closeness and belonging. Sex in public, then, is failed because it is a virtual form of intimacy, grounded in feelings and memories, in shame and loss.

A KXAN NEWS UNDERCOVER

It happens nearly everyday. It is blatant. It is brazen.
—KXAN News, "Sex, Parks, and Videotape"[6]

Although the above transcript excerpt suggests that Austin's KXAN News recognized the everyday character of sex in public in Austin parks, they still treated the sex happening at Bull Creek Park in 2006 as somehow extraordinary. Modeled after the popular NBC show *To Catch a Predator* (*TCAP*), KXAN decided to put Austin "perverts" on notice by going into the park with undercover cameras and then threatening to air the mug shots of the men Austin police later arrested. This threat is in fact an attempt to counter the danger the men frequenting the park instantiate with their transgression of sexual and identitarian norms. As much as the Austin Police Department and the news station hoped to regulate the use of public space, managing the boundaries of who constituted that public was equally important: "Many of these men are married with families. News Thirty-Six is coming back. If we find repeat offenders, we may not use that discretion."[7]

Although they don't explicitly mention it, this manufactured sex panic clearly owes much in its concept and execution to *To Catch a Predator*: an undercover operation into the sexual underbelly of contemporary culture that explicitly and implicitly elevates normative sexuality and resurrects the figure of the pervert from earlier moral panics. In a familiar repetition from earlier sex panics, perversion is twofold: men are having homosexual sex in a public place, and these men are married.[8] But the news channel does not only resurrect the specter of the pervert; it also resurrects the tone of an earlier era in which perverts, then "homosexuals" or "sex deviants," were exposed by the media to a public gaze that effectively imposed a social death sentence, evidenced by firings from jobs, ostracism, and no small number of suicides. These days, being caught can still carry severe penalties, as some states expand the scope of the crimes for which people must register as sex offenders. And while, to my knowledge, no deaths resulted from the KXAN sting, there were also none who protested the production of these men as twenty-first century sex deviants, or the almost extralegal management of their behavior by a local news station.[9]

While the KXAN story uses the undercover strategy of *TCAP* and explicitly mentions online sites such as Squirt.org and Craigslist.org as tied to the problem of public sex, the story is nonetheless quaintly ahistorical, evidencing both amnesia about an earlier wave of stings in 1996 in which more than two hundred men were arrested around Austin parks, and conjuring the figure of the innocent potential victim of lewd and indecent exposure. Like most sex panics, the KXAN news story, along with the earlier *Austin American Statesman* coverage of the

1996 stings, depends on two interrelated and familiar assumptions: that sex out of bounds represents a threat to the public order, and that, in particular, this threat risks the innocence of unwilling witnesses, hikers, dog walkers, neighbors, and above all, children. From the KXAN story:

> Nick has been walking his dog in Bull Creek for nearly twenty years.
>
> He says perverts having public sex in the park has overtaken the beauty. He's worried something worse could happen.
>
> "What's really bad is seeing school buses that pull up here everyday and you know that it's going on right here, and the school bus is oblivious and you see thirty to forty to fifty kids," Nick said.[10]

The implication is clear: the boundaries of the sex public created by the men in the parks risks moving out of the underbrush and potentially incorporating new and even more inappropriate objects of desire. Children who were supposed to commune with Austin's natural beauty may be unwillingly pulled into a sexual jungle of bent desire. This threat is, of course, virtual, triggering anger at the usurpation of public space and anxiety about the safety of children. In part what makes the threat potent is the juxtaposition of a world of nature, the famous Austin green belts of streams, trees, and hiking trails, with sexual acts between men. The former is beautiful, the latter, unnatural, ugly, and dangerous.

Technological contingencies aside, "Sex, Parks, and Videotape" bears more than a passing resemblance to stories that circulated in *The Austin American Statesman* a decade earlier when men were arrested at various parks around Austin, including Bull Creek, during a months-long series of stings. Both stings took place during the era of political correctness, and both are therefore careful not to tie their discourses of perversion too closely to gay identities. As in an editorial that appeared in the *Statesman* in 1996, the KXAN story makes a real effort to decouple perversion from homosexuality. As the 1996 editorial put it, countering claims of entrapment by some gay men,

> Despite protests from some in the gay community, the recent arrests for lewdness and indecent exposure in Austin's Pease Park were not about homosexuality but criminality.

Public sex in a city park is a crime, and it doesn't matter whether that sex is heterosexual or homosexual. All city residents have a right to expect their parks to be free of crime, and that includes the crimes of lewdness and indecent exposure.[11]

Almost ten years later, KXAN likewise conjures a phantasmatic public sphere that includes ordinary law-abiding gays and lesbians (it's all of us, everyone, versus the perverts), noting,

It is predominantly men having sex with men. But let's be clear, this is not a problem exclusive with Austin's gay community.
"No, absolutely not. A lot of the people that we've arrested are professionals. Many of them have ben [sic] married, have children," APD Sergeant Gerardo Gonzalez said.[12]

Though its tone differs significantly, the story reproduces the famous and controversial findings published by Laud Humphreys in *Tearoom Trade,* namely that the men who sought out sex in public with other men were often married and rarely self-identified as gay.[13] Humphrey's work, like Kinsey's earlier studies, suggests that sexual behavior and desires are altogether more fluid than the identity categories that attempt to contain them. The perversion of these men, then, has less to do with the specific acts in which they engaged, than in their transgression of the ostensibly stable lines of identity that puts their proper place at home, with their girlfriends, wives, and innocent kids. By transgressing the norms of identity, belonging, and sexual acts, these men fail to properly belong to the public of which they are a part. And, correspondingly, there's a desire to punish these transgressions (of public and private spheres as well as categories such as gay and straight), a desire that is expressed in the ways all forms of sex in public are positioned as failed forms of intimate belonging. By articulating sex in public as an improper use of public space and a flawed model of sociality, the management and policing of these spaces and practices can be read as an effort to manage the virtuality of both sex and publicness. Both are constituted by excesses: sex by the unconscious or, at least, by the incommensurate or incoherent co-articulation of desire, identity, and practice; and public space by the presence of hidden geographies of desire, largely invisible to the larger non-cruising public. Another way of putting this is to say that much of the larger public demands that cruisers accept the limits (indeed constitutive failures) of normative intimacy, and punishes them when they refuse to accede to this demand by threatening to expose them as (non-gay) queers and perverts.

The threat of the virtual cuts across multiple domains and registers. KXAN threatens exposure; the sex public threatens to incorporate its unwilling witnesses; and virtuality itself threatens to become excessive. If the danger of sexuality rests less in what people actually do than in what they *might* do, then the failure to cinch the virtual's actualization risks wildness, people gone wild with the multiplying pleasures of their bodies.

FALLS FROM GRACE

Maf54 (7:48:00 p.m.): did you spank it this weekend yourself

Xxxxxxxxx (7:48:04 p.m.): no

Xxxxxxxxx (7:48:16 p.m.): been too tired and too busy[14]

The last decade hasn't been kind to conservative homophobes. In the second half of 2006, lurid Instant Messages between Republican congressman Mark Foley and underage congressional pages were leaked to the press. And in November of that year the Reverend Ted Haggard was outed by masseuse and escort Mike Jones, who had had an ongoing relationship with the New Life Church founder. And then, in the summer of 2007, Idaho senator Larry Craig, who had famously called Bill Clinton a "very naughty, nasty boy," threatening to spank him during the Monica Lewinsky scandal, was arrested in the Minneapolis airport after allegedly soliciting an undercover policeman. Each of these men had a record of marginalizing queer desires, bodies, and politics in direct and indirect ways. Foley worked extensively to expand definitions of sexual offenses, especially online; Haggard supported the preemptive Colorado ban on gay marriage; and Craig was likewise an ardent supporter of a federal ban on gay marriage, as well as vigorously pursuing the expulsion of Barney Frank from Congress for his ties to a hustler who briefly operated a prostitution ring out of the congressman's apartment.

Foley and Haggard are implicated not only in forms of sex that fall outside of normative purview, but forms of sex whose impropriety is intensified by their electronic mediation. For Foley, this has to do with the ways his particular behaviors took place largely in digital contexts as well as the first appearance of the story on the blog stops-expredators.com, although as the story unfolded, it became clear that various political figures and media outlets had knowledge of explicit e-mails and instant messages as much as a year earlier. When ABC news confirmed the story, Foley's earlier evasions about his sexual orientation quickly morphed into limited confessions and a hasty resignation. His erstwhile defenders quickly abandoned him, themselves increasingly under scrutiny for what they knew about Foley's actions and when (they'd known quite a bit for quite a long time). The same news outlets that had sat on the Foley story for many months now seized upon the transcripts of Foley's exchanges with young male pages as evidence of political corruption, decadence, and hypocrisy, and as potentially significant in the then upcoming 2006 congressional elections. After his initial denials and subsequent resignation, Foley did little to challenge these characterizations. Indeed, he situated his online activities within a confessional model of culpability in which his transgressive erotic exchanges were the result of abuse and addiction: he was an alcoholic who as an altar boy had been the victim of a priest's sexual interest.

Foley's virtual intimacies, then, were embedded in a broader web of failed social relations: of the betrayal of trust by his childhood priest, the silence of the Republican leadership and news media for whom Foley's homosexuality had been known if not acknowledged for many years, in addition to his invasive (if legally careful)[15] inquiries into the sexual lives of young male pages.

Within religious and political domains, the failures of Foley, Haggard, and Craig have to do with the ways their apparent hypocrisy undermines conservative homophobic sentiment (whether rhetorical or tied to specific policies). Indeed, for Haggard, it is precisely this hypocrisy that undoes him. Two years into their variously transactional and intimate relations, Haggard's masseuse/lover Mike Jones heard Haggard's voice on a television station supporting the Colorado gay marriage ban; Jones subsequently outed Haggard, angered by his hypocrisy.

My own interest in these figures lies less in their hypocrisy than in the ways their stories dramatize and congeal the borders of legitimate relationality and intimacy. Sex with pages, escorts, or anonymous partners emerges as a weak form of intimacy, and these figures' falls then function as cautionary tales about what happens when people get intimacy wrong, misrecognizing one thing (lust or freedom) for another (coupledom or a family). These stories implicitly warn about what happens when sex leaks into the public sphere. Failing to keep intimacy private invites public speculation and censure, which simultaneously constrains and multiplies intimate possibility. These men bear the weight of public shaming, yet at the same time their shaming exposes a larger public to the reality that these forms of transgressive sex are in fact possible (even if also always threatening).

Foley, Craig, and Haggard all failed at concealing their indiscretions, and in the mass-mediated circulation of these failures the scorn and ridicule leveled at these men was tied to the ways their efforts to find connection (through Instant Messages, compensated sex, or in an airport bathroom) were on the wrong side of the real. Indeed, their subjectivities more generally, because they reject homosexuality without shoring up their straightness, remain just over the horizon, in some other speculative space that manages to endlessly delay and defer their queerness. At the same time, these speculations are charged with a life, with potentiality.

By labeling these men sexual hypocrites, the reacting public hoped to snap these figures into preexisting narratives about politics and sexual excess as well as narratives of the closet. Foley willingly participated in this process, proclaiming himself a gay man whose homosexuality was tied to (if not caused by) his victimization as a child and his alcoholism. Haggard and Craig were altogether more resistant, denying at length both their wrongdoing and any potential homosexuality. When, after three weeks of intensive conversion therapy, Haggard reported that he was "completely heterosexual," it was an effort to snuff his delayed and deferred queerness out of existence. Likewise, Craig continued to challenge his conviction and the police policies that target cruisers, while adamantly insisting that he was not gay. All three bought into the publicly circulated (and produced) notion that some forms of intimacy are better than others and that particular forms of sexual contact are practiced by people who are either gay or straight, but not both or neither. The correspondence between their statements and actions and the desires of the witnessing public, however, are not entirely commensurate. The public, of which I am undoubtedly a part, wants more than witnessing or condemnation allows. Our repulsion to these stories is matched if not overwhelmed by our desire to get even closer.

As a public we not only watched these instances of sexual excess and transgression play out in news reports and blogs; we obsessively speculated on them in increasingly proximate ways that implicated our own desires. Our fascination is tied to the specificity of these events: conservatives involved in transgressive sex, online grooming of minors, paid sex, public sex. Others' intimate failures rapturously sweep us away into whole virtual worlds of desire. These worlds might offer exotic escapes from our daily lives (and perhaps the failings of our own intimacies), but they are not unfamiliar even if we might like to disavow their particular content. Indeed, when the Mark Foley news first broke, I found myself unable to read the transcripts of some of the Instant Messages on the ABC Web site. Initially I thought this was because, in an effort to be family friendly, ABC had removed explicit content from their Web site. Later, reading through the strangely unsatisfying, banal, and bizarre text of the messages themselves—the teen talks about his favorite positions to jerk off in and admits to a cast fetish—I realized I had been unable to access the transcripts because ABC's servers had been overwhelmed by the traffic. What struck me was how, for a nation so opposed to underage and intergenerational sex, so many of us were drawn to learn the details of these text messages.

Of course, most people who enter into this world are quick to disavow it. The only pleasure to be taken in the world of online predation must be tied to the narratively powerful fall from grace, rather than the desires the messages express (see my discussion in chapter 4). But the excitement of witnessing the failure can't account for the degree and intensity of speculation and commentary. The public interest in the cases, and especially in their minutiae, suggests that the effort to contain the possibilities these scandals reveal (that one can have sexually explicit chat, sex with pages or escorts, or come on to a cop in an airport bathroom) is simultaneously accompanied by an excess and abundance. Indeed, the public of strangers who read and comment on these cases is drawn into greater proximity not only with one another, but also with the very desires we purport to reject.

TO CATCH A PREDATOR

In 2004, NBC Dateline's *To Catch a Predator* captured the public imagination in a way that other shows that similarly stage the enactment of justice, such as Fox's *Cops,* had not. *TCAP* dramatizes the failures and promises of virtual intimacies: you can meet anyone online, even the jailbait you've been looking for, but at the same time, people online are out to get you; trying to get connected online will lead to failure, yet the spectacle of watching people fail in this way is a huge success, especially in cable reruns.

On the program, volunteer do-gooders from the nonprofit anti–online predator group Perverted Justice troll Internet sites and chat rooms masquerading as sexually precocious underage teens. When men—and there have only been men—contact and engage in sexually explicit talk or try to solicit sex with the imagined minor, they've usually already broken the law. But the show's money shot occurs only after the men agree to meet with the assumed Lolita or Luke, when they arrive at the designated location, and Chris Hansen, *TCAP*'s host, confronts and interviews the would-be child rapist.[16] The men respond in very different ways. Some are defensive, saying they never would have slept with a kid, even though they'd brought a teddy bear along with condoms and lube. Others narrate their own stories of victimization. A couple of years after the show first airs, some even confess to being fans of the program.

TCAP is a testament to the pleasures of looking at the disasters that are other people's intimate lives. And it's a warning to anyone who looks online for intimacy and for parents whose children surf the Net's matrix of desire.

Figuring the Internet as a vast sea of desire and risk, rife with would be predators, *TCAP* broadcasts this drama to the homes of millions of ordinary Americans. The real drama of the show, though, and the key sites for identification or disidentification by viewers center on the failure of these men to direct their erotic energies toward appropriate object choices (adults) in appropriate contexts (the real, not the virtual, world). Their fantasy worlds evidence desire gone awry: looking online for underage victims rather than in the real world for a date, they fail the test of normative relationality, and ultimately they fail as men. The show titillates viewers in part by exploiting the tension between the predators' identities as average guys gone wild and wrong. They're normal, but perverted.

Viewers are thrilled by the discovery that these men—teachers, prosecutors, rabbis, firefighters, tech geeks—have secret lives lived on Web sites and chat rooms, and that beneath their usually unassuming surfaces there are expansive erotic worlds to which, without *TCAP*, we would never gain access. Linda Williams famously coined the phrase "the frenzy of the visible" to describe the visual grammar of pornography.[17] In this instance, though, the source of fear and pleasure lies unseen, in the dangerous desires of the nice neighbor, upstanding community member, and good worker. Hence, the justification of the show, to expose these men to the harsh judgment of public opinion in elaborate setups that provide audiences with the spectacle of the perverts' stunning failures of sociality. The program's voyeurism lies in the way it jumps between scopophilia on the one hand, and the public's erotic rage on the other. Its affective charge emerges in the movement between these positions.

As the series progresses, increasing screen time is spent on the interaction between the "underage" decoy and the men they've invited over:

> Here in New Jersey, where we've set up in a multi-million dollar home on the beach, our decoy Casey is able to have much longer conversations with the men. This gives us a keen insight into what they plan on doing to a young teen. Usually we mostly rely on the men's online chats with Perverted Justice decoys and while that does give us a graphic look at these guy's intentions, it is really startling to see them engage in the grooming process in real-time.

Like the men who are duped into believing that the decoy is a potential eager underage sexual partner, the audience is drawn into the fantasy through these videotaped "longer conversations" and the detailed reflections of the fresh-faced decoy.

By bringing these predators' desires "into the light," *TCAP* triggers a mimetic contagion of desire in which the men, the audience, and the producers of the program are all brought into contact with one another, mirroring one another's longings for illicit sex, punitive retribution, and intimacy's failure. In the following exchange, the host Chris Hansen repeats snippets of Anthony Palumbo's online conversation:

> Hansen: You asked him in your chat if he was top or bottom. What does that mean?
>
> Palumbo: Did I ask? I don't remember though.
>
> Hansen: Are you top or bottom?
>
> Hansen: I'm horny, you said.

Palumbo: I was just fooling around.

Hansen: Well, if you're just fooling around, why were you so concerned about knowing whether or not he was a cop?

Palumbo: Just joking.

Hansen: Just joking.[18]

On *TCAP*, viewers can experience the pleasure of taboo desires while shielding themselves from the scope or consequences of their own nascent predatory feelings. The show casts the sexual worlds of predators as transgressive and virtual, as beyond the pale of the norm and of the real, but the resulting intimacy suggests something altogether more.

By staging intimacy gone wrong, and suturing danger, risk, and failure to virtual spaces, *TCAP* also sends clear messages about how togetherness is done right. And this right form of intimacy is itself perversely the image of the couple or the family witnessing the program, sharing the fascination and contempt for the failed intimacies the show concocts. If the men on *TCAP* all get caught, the desires of the audience remain altogether uncaptured. Whether watching the program or reading the extended chat logs at pervertedjustice.com, viewers and potential predators alike can immerse themselves in worlds of underage sex, even if the warning about different sorts of capture, that is, getting busted, is clear.

If intimacy is conceived as failed or virtual when it is linked to sex in public or online predation, it is also marked by a structuring excess, namely the field of potential desires from which these anonymous, spectacular, transgressive, or abject scenes are drawn. Failed intimacies, as sex, closeness, or belonging, are reminders both of the limits of normative sex and sexuality and that nonnormative intimacies are available, if at a cost. A virtual intimacy does not, after all, collapse all desires or encounters that are not socially sanctioned into a sort of abyss; rather, it actualizes some intimacies as more or less desirable and dangerous than others. In so doing, of course, failure itself becomes a relative term (as I hope I have indicated throughout this chapter). Failure is not an extinction of the possible, not a dead end. Instead, failure frames the possible in negative terms without actually erasing all possibilities. Indeed, many of the ideas that circulate about sex in public, such as the moralizing that constitutes the scopophilia of a sex scandal, heightens the awareness that possibilities accrete to failures. Typically, failure is wielded as a weapon—it's a loser's just dues and a warning for the rest of us to stay on our toes. In this way, the commonsensical antipathy toward public sex, sexual hypocrisy, or virtual sex works to foreclose the possibilities for queer and other, alternative intimacies to take form. Indeed, sensationalistic moralizing in particular seems to have very little do with intimacy at all, encouraging instead the alienation of perverts and the rest of us insofar as it inculcates a pervasive, fearful sense of being watched, of having one's own desires endlessly subjected to some regulatory norm. At the same time, these failures are enormously generative. For some, like Fred, failure affords a space to cultivate more nourishing forms of sociality. Then there's the pleasure to be had in failure, in the carnal sort that comes with hooking up in meat space or online (outside or on the side of the couple form), and in watching the trainwrecks of others' intimate lives. And in failing to live up to norms of intimacy, cruisers, Republicans, and even creepy online fantasists remind people of the virtual trajectories their intimate lives *might* take.[19]

What comes after failure? Within contemporary U.S. national culture, bootstrap ideologies suggest and encourage failures to try again. But giving up is an option too.

CHAPTER TWO

Intimacies in the Multi(player)verse

In the overlapping fandoms of comic and gaming culture, a multiverse is comprised of many existing, sometimes overlapping, parallel universes. In different genres of fiction, these are speculative zones that allow creators and fans to ask and explore "What if?" scenarios in which they creatively reframe familiar characters, spaces, and relationships. To take a famous example from the world of DC Comics, in one universe Superman is married to Lois Lane and in another to Lana Lang. Sometimes an apparently minor difference can have significant, indeed, world-altering effects. And, of course, sometimes things bleed through, as when Bizarro Superman wreaks havoc in the world of the Superman we've grown used to. In another example, Philip K. Dick's famous novel *Man in the High Castle*, the Axis Powers, having won World War II, exercise their hegemony in a conquered United States, which has been divided into puppet states governed by Japan and Germany. Now, a multiverse isn't simply a flight of fancy, as any good geek will tell you.[1] More to the point, game designers have drawn on Neal Stephenson's similar notion of the metaverse, first articulated in his novel *Snow Crash*: a virtual space in which a world operates as a metaphor and where humans interact with one another in the form of avatars. Although the idea of the multiverse stretches the Deleuzean notions of the virtual that inform much of my thinking, it is nonetheless also possible to think of the virtual as the actual's multiple, mirror image; prior to its capture (when one relates a memory or a narrative of identity), the virtual is multiple, existing in many different states in a plane of immanence.

Here, I use this notion of the multiverse as a way to think through the different ways intimacies materialize in the massively multiplayer online game (MMOG), *The World of Warcraft* (*WoW*). *WoW* is multiple in many ways, not least of which because it is an actualization of not one, but many virtual worlds: the worlds of the fantasy, which inform its geography and play style, as well as the worlds of the millions of users who play it everyday. In what follows, I track notions of multiplicity and play in both dominant and minor forms of intimacy in *Warcraft*. In the first half of this chapter, I identify two of the most common forms of intimacy in the game world, group and solo play. While arguing that these forms of intimacy are largely instrumental, figuring sociality as a means to an end, I also begin to recuperate their immanent multiplicity through the intimate incursions gamers have made into *WoW*'s narrative universe and how they extend these intimacies toward other, more profligate ends. In the final section of the chapter, I use these forms of belonging and touch that escape instrumentality to figure virtual intimacy in a modestly hopeful register as a means *without* an end.

INSTRUMENTAL INTIMACIES IN AZEROTH

An elf was following me, annoyingly, repeatedly asking variations of the same questions:

"Will you be my friend?"

"Do you know where the druid is?"

"How do I get the quest?"

"Will you help me?"

"Invite me to a group?"

"Don't you want to be my friend?"

Finally, I'd had enough. "NO!" I shouted, "Leave me alone!"

Another nearby elf, laughing, intervened: "Why don't you just ignore him?"

After dragging my mouse over a series of interface options on my computer screen, I finally found what I was looking for. I pressed the "ignore" button and typed in my pursuer's screen name. The elf's speech bubbles stopped appearing, although he kept following me around for a while, standing in front of me and jumping up and down to try and get my attention again. Eventually he lost interest and wandered off, while I went about finishing my quest.

At my keyboard, I found myself anxious and frustrated. What was I supposed to do? Should I have talked with him longer or become his friend? After all, I had many of the same questions. I didn't know what I was doing in this new world; I barely understood how to move my avatar around. I was just following the advice of one of my students: "Just go around and click on the people with exclamation points over their heads. They're going to tell you what to do and where to go. Start there."

Beginning in the spring of 2007, at the urging of students, colleagues, and friends who were familiar with my interest in virtual intimacies, I downloaded a free trial of *The World of Warcraft* and began playing. Though I had occasionally played computer games as a child and adolescent, I don't identify as a gamer. Two weeks later, at the end of the free trial period and, I had assumed, my experiment with this virtual world, I dutifully entered my credit card information to activate a monthly subscription. "I need to do much more research," I told myself. It didn't hurt, of course, that I found the game enjoyable, or that the social networks it enabled, with my students and friends who played, opened up new opportunities for thinking through digitally mediated relationships. Indeed, many of those who encouraged me to immerse myself in *Warcraft* became my chief interlocutors, generously sharing their own histories with the game, as well as advice and support (and occasionally even a little in-game gold) as I tackled learning everything from basic keyboard commands, to traveling, to the game's sophisticated and massive economy.

Now, years later, I can't claim to have ever mastered *WoW,* although I have logged thousands of hours in game. Indeed, I play only sporadically now, during summers or when I teach a particular course. But I'm still thrilled when I game, although this excitement is only rarely tinged with the confused anxiety that marked my early weeks of play. Rather, it is the charge that comes with the feeling that when I log on, I enter a social world.

THE WORLD OF WARCRAFT

The World of Warcraft is an elaborate fantasy playscape that takes as its inspiration fantasy literature such as Tolkien's *The Lord of the Rings* and role-playing games like *Dungeons & Dragons.* First released in 1994 as the real-time strategy game *Warcraft: Orcs & Humans,* it was

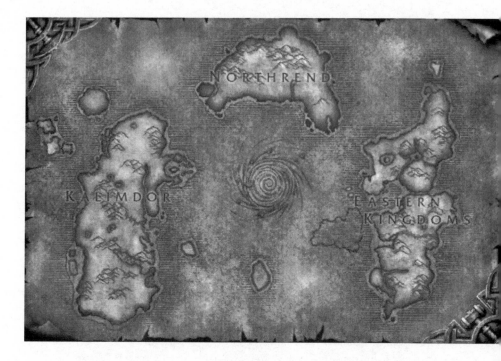

FIGURE 2.1. A map of the World of Warcraft as of the Cataclysm Expansion (this does not include the remnants of the Dranei planet known as Outland on which gameplay also occurs).

reintroduced as a massively multiplayer online game in 2004, going on to become, as of this writing, the most successful online role-playing game of its kind, with more than ten million players worldwide who pay subscription fees to play. As an MMOG, players do not just navigate the game content on their own, or with one or two other players, but rather with thousands of others.[2]

Warcraft is set in the worlds of Azeroth and Outland, two planets with expansive geographies as well as complex environmental and cultural ecologies (Fig. 2.1). Entering the game is not unlike entering a large-scale, historical role-playing game rendered in compelling three-dimensional graphics, though without the dice or the physical proximity afforded by games such as *Dungeons & Dragons* or by live action role playing (LARPing). Depending on the sort of character one creates, new users view a short narrative film that situates the particular race they have chosen in the game's larger narrative universe of the game. When, for example, I first created Ophele on the Aggramar server several years ago, this is the story that oriented me to the world and to her particular embeddedness within it, narrated in the gravelly, dramatic voice of movie previews:

> *For nearly seven thousand years, the High Elves cultivated a shining magical kingdom, hidden deep within the forests of northern Lordaeron. But five years ago, the undead Scourge invaded Quel-Thalas and drove the elves to the brink of extinction. Led by the evil death knight Arthus, the Scourge destroyed the mystical Sunwell, thereby severing the elves from the source of their arcane power. Although the scars of that conflict are evident, the remaining elves have banded together and retaken much of their homeland. Calling themselves Blood Elves, these grim survivors are committed to regaining the vast powers they once commanded. Inspired by the leadership of their beloved prince, Kael'thas Sunstrider, the Blood Elves now seek new sources of arcane magic and the means of defending their land against the undying horrors of the Scourge. As one of the few surviving Blood Elves, you must master your thirst for magic and shape the destiny of your people.*

Again, this oriented me toward the story of the Blood Elves, but it also oriented me in the larger, then thirteen-year-old, densely storied world of *Warcraft*. This larger narrative is worth describing in greater detail because it is so elaborately developed, and, more importantly, in the context of the MMOG, because it implicitly situates the player in relationship to other players. From the moment I created Ophele the Blood Elf, I had a history, to my enemies the Undead Scourge as the story above notes, but also to other elves, to humans, demons, and so on. And many of these others, I knew, would be animated by other people, people I would come to encounter in the world.

At first glance, the story *Warcraft* tells might appear familiar to anyone with even passing knowledge of the tropes of epic fantasy: a long-running conflict between the forces of good and evil. In this instance, The Alliance and The Horde represent these forces, respectively. Since the introduction of the first *Warcraft* game in 1994, the story of the planet Azeroth has been consistently expanded with new games and, more recently with "The Burning Crusade," "The Wrath of the Lich King," and in December 2010 "Cataclysm." These "expansion packs" create new content, open up new areas of the world, and afford users the opportunities to utilize new races and character classes. In earlier iterations, the Alliance was initially figured as a band of heroic humans who fought bloodthirsty orcs. Yet, the story became increasingly more complex, especially as gamers began to play other races rather than merely fight them. The orcs, it turned out, were not initially a violent culture, but a shamanic one that had been enslaved by the demonic powers of the Burning Legion. They eventually freed themselves from the Legion's demonic influence and redeemed themselves through the sacrifice of one of their great leaders, who gave his life to destroy one of the demon lords. In "The Burning Crusade," Alliance and Horde work together (though they are still opposed in other ways) to fight invading demons in the landscape of the Outland, the fragments of a destroyed planet held together by the magic of the Twisting Nether.

Each playable race likewise has a story, and it is a truncated version of this story that players encounter when they first create a new character. I've mentioned only a small portion of the stories of three of the twelve playable races, and my own narrative barely scratches the surface of the storytelling at work in constructing the world of Azeroth, a world collectively imagined and constructed by thousands of people for more than fifteen years across the different media of computer and card games, comics, novelizations, and, soon, feature films. All of this is to point to the ways identity in this muli(player)verse is constructed like those in the worlds we typically navigate: many aspects of our identities are preformed for us, situating and binding us to the narratives of the past, to inheritances of class, gender, and race, as well as to particular constellations of intimacy.

CONSTRAINING PLAY

Part of *WoW*'s pleasure has to do with the way the world's expansive and elaborate scale affords opportunities for creative exploration, an exploration made vital with a promise of freedom from the doldrums of everyday life. Indeed, "explorers" are the sorts of gamers who "come to see what is [in a world] and to map it for others. They are happiest with challenges that involve the gradual revelation of the world. They want the world to be very big, and filled with hidden beauty that can only be unlocked through persistence and creativity."[3] I found the scope of exploration seductive, and the spaces, cities, and landscapes evidenced a sophisticated philosophy of design. The architecture of Silvermoon City and the forests of Lordaeron were inspiring, and I was amazed that Ophele could move through these spaces in a way that reflected their scale; running or, later, riding a range of mounts, required patience as well, since it took time, sometimes lots of it, to traverse these virtual geographies. As well, the more she accomplished, that is, as she leveled up, the farther she could travel, and the more of the world I could see through her eyes. This movement moved me; it affected me in the sharp contrast it offered to my other, also recently adopted, home in upper Manhattan. Exploring this fantasy world was a welcome respite from my new responsibilities as a full-time professor and a pleasurable escape from an inhospitable New York winter.

Yet, even as this experience of encountering the "hidden beauty" of the world was affecting, I also learned that *WoW* is also a profoundly *closed system* insofar as game developers, programmers, and administrators set the terms and limits of gameplay, effectively producing particular forms of intimacy as more or less important to the world. These limits became apparent when, in my early travels, I tried unsuccessfully to go places that looked interesting; Ophele would simply stop, as if encountering an invisible wall. This world had scale, but not infinite scale, and its scope was subject to rules other than my own desires.

FIGURE 2.2. Character creation. One of the first screen new gamers view. Here, a male Draenei Shaman has been selected.

From the point of view of character creation (Fig. 2.2), users' choices are constrained by sex, race, and class (though not in the usual sense meant by academics who use these words, or certainly not only). That is, users can choose to belong to one of the two factions, Horde or Alliance, they can choose to be either male or female, and select from different races.[4] And while gamers can and do create multiple characters, once they create an avatar they cannot significantly modify it except by leveling up, adding equipment such as armor or weapons, or by paying a small fee in an in-game "barbershop" in which they can change minor details such as hair style and skin tone; they cannot change their gender or adjust the laughably exaggerated sexual dimorphism of their avatars.

Equipment and weapons, or "gear," are virtual items players use to equip their characters, and which make possible and improve game play. Gear is essential for an enjoyable experience in game. Without it, it's not possible to move beyond particular areas or defeat monsters (although players' avatars are essentially immortal, resurrecting when they are killed). As players quest and obtain experience, they "level up," becoming more powerful and enabling them to acquire more health (more health means surviving battles longer), advanced gear, and travel to more places. The necessity of leveling up and acquiring gear represents, then, another central constraint.

Finally, given the time necessary to level up and equip a character, or to reach endgame content (currently level 85 with the new expansion set), most casual gamers focus on one or two avatars or "toons" at a time. This is in large part because, as anthropologist Tom Boellstorff observes in his study of another virtual world, *Second Life,* time resists virtualization in ways that space does not. Entering into a virtual world does not also mean one enters a virtual, otherworldly time even if the experience of time *appears* to contract or expand. A day does not suddenly become twenty-six hours, and there are only so many hours a day in which one can play the game. Hence, temporality is another central limit to gameplay.[5]

CONSTRAINING BELONGING

The cooperation in games such as *Warcraft* and other MMOGs represents a shift in the history of gaming. Indeed, this shift came with earlier games, though not "massively multiplayer," in the role-playing communities found in MOOs and MUDs, and some games on the

Game Boy console; these represented key imaginative and technological changes in game play.[6] While most games that allowed players to play simultaneously pitted gamers in battles against one another, most of the new generation of online role-playing games have built collaboration into the architecture of the game world.[7]

Just as characters have choices about the sorts of avatars they might become, they have choices about the sorts of intimacies they might engage in. But these choices are largely limited by the game's overall structure. Being with others is conceived as essential to gameplay in *WoW* but it is also constrained or channeled into very particular forms of relation and tied to achievement. Though distinct from other games in the sense that it requires collaboration, *WoW* is still a game that abides by a logic of success and failure.

In the remainder of the chapter, I focus on two of the most common forms of intimacy in *Warcraft,* group and solo play. I suggest that most forms of intimacy in *Warcraft* are instrumental; intimacy functions as a necessary means to an end, and that end is advancement according to the logic of game play. In this way, *Warcraft* reproduces intimacy in ways that have by now become familiar: namely, as a normative script in which one's connectedness is constrained by normative aspirations and ideals, especially to forms of material success.

PLAYING WITH OTHERS

As I have argued elsewhere in this book, intimacy figures centrally in narratives of a life lived right. Outside of the intimate life dwell the lonely, the abject, and the queer. What critiques of solo play highlight is the sensibility that playing by or with oneself casts aside the responsibility *to be in relation with others.* One of the responsibilities of a human life lived right is an obligation toward intimacy. This imperative to be intimate is, of course, only one way in which a meaningful or proper life is produced through different vectors of culpability, through responsibility and obligation to others, or the demand to be intimate. Genuinely solo play, I have argued, is exceedingly rare in *WoW,* and the rules of the game world itself do not allow for an absolute rejection of all forms of culpable sociality. In fact, the life of an avatar in *WoW* looks a lot like the idealized life path set out for most of us. The noob, or "newbie," leaves childish things, such as undirected play and exploration, behind; the player gets a job, participating in the economy, consuming, producing, and saving resources; s/he engages ideologies of achievement and merit, in which gear functions as both material and symbolic capital; and, perhaps most importantly, s/he produces a largely persistent and stable identity, one that is projected as more or less reputable and dependable.

While it is possible to advance in the game without interacting with others, in general players must work with other players. In early play, other gamers, along with official and unofficial online forums and wikis, aid the noob in learning the lay of the land. This is done by using in-game chat channels, including private and public chat, as well as by using a range of add-ons built into the game or provided by third parties.

As a gamer advances, this need for instrumental intimacy intensi-fies; there are many quests that only a very few players could manage to accomplish on their own, or "do solo." Moreover, much of the most useful (and cool) gear come from multiplayer "instanced dungeons," advanced areas in which "elite" monsters are harder to kill and the loot is much better. Insofar as instances are designed for multiplayer groups, typically for groups of five, ten, twenty-five, and up to as many as forty players, it's essential that one engage with others, cooperating toward a shared goal: again, more and better stuff.

Even as group play is constructed as essential to successful game-play this does not mean that its instrumentalization results in the desired ends. Although Blizzard has with recent expansions and updates corrected one of the most frustrating elements of group play—the need to wait in queues or actively seek out other gamers for instance, an often time-consuming process—finding other players is no guarantee of success. Even as groups are automatically constituted, players come with widely different levels of experience. Because classes of characters are intended to play highly specific roles, these differences in experience can mean success or failure in a dungeon. Moreover, these play groups are fragile. If a particularly self-interested gamer accomplishes the goals or quests s/he has entered the dungeon for, or if mom calls a player to dinner, then players sometimes simply disappear, leaving the group a player or more short. And although groups can sometimes continue without one member, at other times this is not possible and the team will need to wait until a replacement can be found or end its efforts.

Nonetheless, given the ways instances are so important to the overall experience of the game—they provide cooperative opportu-nities to obtain experience, gold, and gear—most players suffer the frustrations of the process even as considerable drama can ensue. In earlier incarnations of the game, players were frustrated when they were removed from groups as more desirable players (or friends of group members) were identified and invited into the group.[8]

Group leaders are empowered to add and delete players from groups. Being removed from a group, or "booted," is not an uncommon experience, as most gamers will attest. It is also often very frustrating for those who have waited to join a group only to be kicked out with little or no explanation: "needed a higher level toon," "gotta have heals," "sorry my friend wanted to join." While it's customary to provide some sort of rationale, it is by no means universal. Being kicked out of a group "feels a bit like being dumped," as if one's avatar, and by extension, oneself, had not yet reached an appropriate developmental stage or level of success. The disappointment that accompanies the rejection is often paired with anger as well, not just at the group leader who did the booting, but toward gamers who approach the play experience as a set of calculations, thereby "perverting" the ethos of fun that draws players to the game in the first place.[9]

Although friendships can and do form from instanced groups, it's just as common that experiences in a group might help one identify players to avoid in the future. Given the rationale with which many players approach the necessary intimacy of instanced groups, it's not surprising that these relationships are temporary and tenuous, highlighting as well the ways that intimacy is a form of relating constructed in part through "tacit obligations to remain unproblematic."[10] Instrumental gamers frequently ignore the protests of those they've booted from a group; indeed, they ignore all but the most necessary communication. Another gamer is, for these players, simply another tool, along with their weapons and gear, to help them achieve what they want. Self-interestedly determined to actualize their own potential, the instrumental gamers permit only those forms of communication and togetherness that make the fewest demands on them. And most gamers, although they complain loudly and frequently about the struggle to work with others (especially, though not always, with strangers), have little hope that these temporary forms of belonging will be constructed otherwise.

GUILDS

One way in which even casual players do manage to more easily form groups for dungeons is by belonging to a guild. Guilds are much larger groups that gamers can become a part of (sometimes easily and sometimes only through an occasionally complex application process). Of varying sizes and durations, guilds sometimes attract only a handful of players and last for a few days or weeks, while others may have hundreds of players. Some, like The Tribe on the Aggramar server, have existed since the game's earliest online version. Like regular team play, guilds benefit players by providing material resources: money, advice, gear, and cooperation. Belonging to a guild also makes things such as raids possible, in which groups of as many as forty players team together to fight powerful monsters. Raids provide "legendary" equipment dropped by a slain endgame monster that is usually awarded to players based on a complex system of points.

Insofar as guilds provide opportunities for players to assemble groups and complete challenging quests, guilds are effectively an extension of the instrumental forms of intimacy I have discussed thus far. Yet unlike instanced group play in which gamers assemble a small group of players they may have played with before or whom they select randomly for a few hours at a time, the duration of some established guilds provides opportunities for other, multiple forms of intimacy to emerge (a point I elaborate in greater detail below). But in brief, the public of a guild allows many different forms of contact and encounter to blossom between players, certainly including those modes of intimacy that simply allow players to "get things done," but that can also transform into on- and offline friendship and romance.[11]

While many media accounts focus on the dangers online games like *Warcraft* pose to relationships (see, for example, the mini-docs such as "Warcrack" found on YouTube and the documentary *Second Skin*), there are as well many accounts of intimacies that begin in the game world.[12]

For others, though, *WoW* relationships, which have produced lively discussion threads on blogging sites such as LiveJournal, are simply embedded within larger contexts of love and relating. In one LiveJournal thread, for example, a user laments the ways she and her boyfriend are framed, respectively, as slut and homewrecker, after she and her former undead warlock boyfriend broke up. The post, tantalizingly headlined "Looking for love in all the wrong 'races,'" highlights the ways relationships that begin in game mirror many of the complexities that couples face in their everyday lives offline.

I am an undead warlock and 2 years ago, while playing with my favorite guild, I met a fellow undead warlock who lived rather close to me. We got to talking and ended up really liking each other. We had a great 2 year relationship which ended a few months back when we decided we were leading different lifestyles and it was best to just be friends.

This is where it gets a little weird for most people. After we had broken up, another undead warlock in a guild I had recently joined started talking to me. He definitely sparked my interest and somehow we hit it off (even though he lives across the country from me). We didn't tell anyone because my ex was in the same guild with us, and we all knew how much drama that would cause. Eventually, my ex decided that he would quit before the rumors would start to spread and it would get too uncomfortable for him to play (it's not like he cared much for the game anyway).

Soon enough people were finding out and while some didn't care, even my friends were saying really random things. It goes from silly things like "oh well, now I know who's the better warlock" and "lol, you soul drained your ex" to bad things like "sloppy seconds" and "how does it feel to have your [censored] tossed around between all the [undead] locks in the game." A lot of people felt "disappointed" in me, as if I did something really wrong (maybe they think I cheated on my ex for him, but I'm not sure). A lot of people think I'm just weird and way too into the game. (http://community.livejournal.com/wow_ladies/5346472.html)

Here, what is initially the amicable ending of one relationship and the beginning of another is filtered through the same misogynist worldview familiar to middle schoolers and feminist theorists alike, one that identifies women who have more than one relationship as sluts. Certainly, I don't intend to valorize this worldview, but both the sexist language and the therapeutic self-expression of these experiences are characteristic of larger cultural values and patterns pertaining to intimacy. Outside of taking place in virtual contexts, what is it that makes this sort of relationality virtual? For the poster, at least, the distinction likely does little to mitigate her feelings of victimization.

In a very different context, anthropologists Daniel Miller and Don Slater suggest in their essay "Relationships" that computer-mediated communications are simply more recent iterations of established cultural patterns of relating. They make this argument not to counter the widespread belief that somehow virtual technologies or communications are somehow less real than other, face-to-face means of communication, or that virtual technologies are in fact real, but, instead, to argue that the opposition of real and virtual is a kind of theoretical and methodological dead end. As they put it, "the opposition of real and virtual . . . completely misses the complexity and diversity of relationships that people may pursue through the communicative media that they embed in their ongoing social lives."[13] It's not hard to agree that relationships are complex and diverse, or to critique casual oppositions of the real and virtual. Here, Miller and Slater ignore the historical and philosophical articulations of the virtual as an ideal space of potential, which nonetheless has meaningful and concrete effects. They also miss the ways intimacy is always already virtual, tied to fantasy and longing, but also enabled through forms of presence that can be intensified by distance as much as by proximity.[14]

One way the shared experience of presence is produced in *WoW* guilds is through some prior affiliations and affinities. While many guilds attract users because of their size and longevity, some users employ other, identitarian means to identify and assemble guilds. Sara Andrews, in a story widely reported in media sources such as the BBC and the online technology magazine CNET.com, used an in-game chat channel to seek members to join her GLBT-friendly guild, Oz. An administrator initially threatened to close her account if she did not cease her solicitation of guild members, which the administrator claimed violated Blizzard's anti-harassment policy.[15] Andrews challenged the threatened ban, in part citing the hypocrisy of using an anti-harassment policy to ban behavior whose end result would have been to create a harassment-free environment in a game world where "gay" and "fag" are two of the most widely and casually circulated epithets. Andrews's rejection of the administrator's logic, as well as the swift response by gay activists, gamers, and media, led Blizzard to offer her a formal apology and provide sensitivity training to its game administrators. Yet since then, only a handful of explicitly GLBT guilds have emerged, including Stonewall Alliance and Spreading Taints.

THE DEATH OF THE AMAZONS

As of this writing, my highest level toon, my Blood Elf rogue Ophele, still belongs to The Amazons of Kalimdor, a GLBT-friendly guild on the Aggramar server. The Amazons is a female toon–only guild, meaning that while men and women can belong to the guild, they can only do so if they game with a female avatar. My earliest *WoW* interlocutor recommended this guild to me, and after much trepidation about joining a guild at all, I finally contacted one of the guild officers and became a part of this small, close-knit group. I enjoyed my short time in this guild and found all of its members very helpful in learning to play in what is, as I've indicated, a very sophisticated virtual world. Yet, the guild has died; it's relatively small member base increasingly pushed more members to join other guilds where they can find more people to play with. A handful of players, myself included, remained for a while, attached in different ways and for different reasons (female empowerment, nostalgia) to this group of Amazons. Speaking with other guild members before and after they've left for other guilds, they described a sense of loss characteristic to intimacy, or rather, to its absence or failure. As in other instances in which a closely knit group comes undone, ongoing feelings of connectedness and belonging mark the power of the intimate to endure: "I had to move my toon to another guild. It just wasn't possible to do some of the really advanced stuff in the game. But I keep an alt [alternative avatar] here and check in. It's nice to know there are still some people trying to keep it alive." On the one hand, this guild member's story indicates the ways that feelings of shared belonging caved in and gave way to instrumental forms of play. Yet, the fact that she continues to keep an "alt," a secondary, often lower-level character, in the guild attests to her ongoing attachment to this fierce group of female toons.

SOLO PLAY

Solo play represents the other dominant mode of intimacy in *WoW*. In this case, however, intimacy refers not to a feeling of shared belonging but to that which is "most inward," those qualities of selfhood that are essential, persistent, and often hidden from others, the "'inner-self' [that] is not defined by achievements or knowledge or accomplishments but rather by the personal style of our approach to existence."[16]

Within the context of the game world, many players spend most of their time working on their own, in the repetitive destruction of mobs or skill training known as "grinding," only occasionally working with others whether in or outside the context of a guild. Indeed, while players alone cannot obtain much of the choicest gear in solo play, they can accomplish a good deal: after two or three or six or ten hours of play, a gamer can earn money and acquire gear and loot without ever needing to engage another person.

Although profoundly productive, even necessary, for success in the game, playing solo is precisely the sort of play most frequently identified as dangerous in everyday discussions and in media accounts. When media refer to MMOGs like *WoW,* solo play figures as central in narratives of gamers gone wild. In these discourses, solo play represents intimacy not in its normative form, as a mode of relating with others, but in its pathological form as an excessive inwardness, an inside gone rotten. This has been famously documented and widely reported in the case of a South Korean man who died of exhaustion in 2005 after fifty hours of nearly continuous play.[17] The trope has become increasingly well-worn: long hours of solo play have led to alienation and a disavowal of the ordinary world in favor of a more pleasurable and immersive one, one in which it's possible to be both engaged and in control in ways distinct both from many of the demands of everyday life by work or family and from interactions with other forms of media. This is intimacy figured as an especially hazardous form of masturbation, as nonreproductive, obsessive, and narcissistic, the turning over of the self to a machine.

This is the form of play associated with *otaku,* a Japanese term used to describe hardcore gamers and fans. Increasingly the term has gained purchase in the United States, though some of its specific valences have been lost. In Japan, the term has both positive and negative meanings, referring to the "the national obsession with techno-constructed realties" that is a source of pride and accomplishment for many Japanese, and the ways that "*otaku* [have] also been associated with pathology and violence."[18] In the United States, *otaku* is an increasingly self-employed term gamers and fans use to describe their financial and affective investments, as well as their frequently stigmatized behavior. Worn as a badge of honor, American *otaku,* including hardcore *WoW* gamers, illustrate a new cultural sensibility in which "geek is the new chic."[19]

The trope of technologically produced atomism isn't a new one of course, and is tied to longstanding narratives about the depersonalizing, addictive qualities of all technology and media. What's especially noteworthy about how these discourses circulate around *WoW* and other games, however, is the way that they are so frequently tied to relationality:

"Say goodbye to your boyfriend for a month or two."

"The computer made us break up."

"He'd rather play the game than have sex with me."

The danger of gaming, it seems, is that the pleasure (usually male) gamers experience in their intimacy with the game world will exceed the pleasure they take with their other relationships, including what should be their most significant ones. While implicit in the many political efforts to frame games as dangerous, efforts that rely on particular understandings of the mimetic power of game violence, others, such as those posted by the founders of the *WoW* Widows group at Yahoo! and Gamerwidow.com, make the threat games pose more explicit:

> Gamer Widow is a term for those who have a relationship with a Gamer (one who plays video games, be it on a console or on the computer) who pays more attention to the game than to their partner . . . thereby making their partner a "gamer widow" (female) or "gamer widower" (male). In general we say "gamer widow" and encompass both male and female community members.
>
> GamerWidow.com is a place for all sorts of Gamer Widow(er)s to come together and discuss their experiences, learn about other "widows" and also learn about the games that their gamers are obsessed with. Gamers who want to quit or are trying to quit or want to learn more about us are also welcome! (http://www.gamerwidow.com/)

Curiously, the founders of these sites seem to miss the point that many critics of online sociality make, namely, that online sociality is itself inherently lacking or addictive or atomizing. Arguably, they have simply enabled another sort of virtual intimacy: the fantasy of a community that will, miraculously, never tire of one's complaining.

Central to the anxieties surrounding solo play, then, is the frightening notion that one can be intimate with a machine and with oneself and leave other people behind altogether. Of course, this might be quite utopic for some who prefer the feelings of achievement and power they obtain in a virtual world, or for others for whom most human relationships are altogether too awkward or constraining. Anne Allison, describing conditions of life in millennial Japan, calls this "intimate alienation," an experience of "connected disconnectedness."[20] In *WoW,* playing solo is still to play with others; even if one avoids communication or cooperation, other gamers will continue to share the same world. At the same time, this experience of connected disconnectedness, in which users are proximate to one another yet simultaneously distant, is tied to the ways solo gamers create a world of their own choosing, or, rather, put the world to their own uses. In fact, the many thousands of players in a realm, whether or not they play together, effectively create their own worlds, transforming each realm into a multiverse. Gamers' experiences bond them to the world in unique ways, surely, but they are also creating private worlds, singular "fenced-in paradises," within the broader public.[21]

INTIMACY AND MULTIPLICITY

Thus far, I have largely focused on intimacies as they function in the context of *WoW*'s game world, although in important ways, these intimacies have already been seen to exceed the limits of the game world (in the death of the South Korean man or among *WoW* widows). As well, I have described how game intimacies are instrumental or transactional, arguing that they are essentially means to an end, namely, in game material and symbolic success and power. Here, I want to examine some of the ways other, perhaps less instrumental, intimacies emerge in the bleed between actual and virtual, as well as the ways they can jump from one world to another, propagate, and multiply.

NAKED NIGHT ELVES

In one of my earliest experiences as a *WoW* noob, I witnessed a parade of nearly naked, dancing night elves. Even though I had spent time in other virtual spaces such as AIM and the chatrooms at Gay.com where sex and corporeality were very much foregrounded, I was not yet equipped with the conceptual tools to make this encounter meaningful. I certainly didn't grasp what appropriate comportment looked like in this virtual world as compared to those others, where "sup" and "a/s/l" (age/sex/location) might be the extent of one's (pre-sex) encounter. Was it, for example, appropriate to remove most of one's clothing to experiment with different looks? If I could get naked, could I also have sex?

While I came to learn that this parade of dancing, nearly naked night elves was likely a group of devoted Horde players looking to have a little fun at the expense of Alliance players (Night elves, are, again, one of the races that make up The Alliance) before engaging in a raid,[22] the event still stands as a reminder of the embodied anxiety I frequently experienced when I first began to play, as well as the confusion I felt about in-game propriety and etiquette. Now, though, I think of these things—my anxiety and confusion as well as the thrill of seeing naked digital bodies—as the sorts of more corporeal forms of contact the game affords. Indeed, users have shown creativity and resourcefulness in creating erotic lives in a world that doesn't, strictly speaking, enable eroticism between avatars. One's avatar can point, wave, sit, kneel, laugh out loud, purr, flirt, and even kiss, but not fuck. Users, though, in playful and sometimes inspired ways, have made use of chat and voice features to have liaisons in and out of character, as well as in and out of world. Indeed, as scholars of virtual worlds have observed, and as the stories about relationships I discuss above illustrate, in-game encounters and romances can lead to face to face encounters and real world intimacies: from just fooling around to marriage.[23]

Two other examples are illustrative here: one, an interlocutor's narrative about a truncated real world encounter, the other, a thwarted rendezvous between two Night Elves in the game. In the first instance, a gamer who helped me navigate much of my early experiences in *WoW* described how an in-game relationship characterized by flirtation and, eventually, by more erotic exchanges in private chat channels, led to an in-person encounter. Unlike some stories that circulate about marriages that result from in-game relationships, in this instance, although they met at a hotel, their relationship remained unconsummated—their chemistry in the game didn't translate; they "just didn't feel it."

The other encounter, also marked by failure, is altogether more dramatic even though it takes place entirely in *WoW*. Using an underground tram to travel between two major cities, a dwarf named Gedran accidentally discovers two nude Night Elves engaged in a tryst in the seclusion of the tramline corridors. Importantly, this event takes place on a Role-Playing (RP) server in which users speak and act in accordance with their avatars' identities. The dwarf, upon seeing the couple, jumps from the tram and hides behind a pillar, still privy to the intimate conversation (really, they're "emoting," a type of textual inter- action where an /e command allows the character to communicate in "emotions" rather than "chat") taking place between the two elves:

> Artemisa groans softly, biting your neck softly, her breath hard against your neck, "Oh . . ."

> Inotep smiles and his fingers move in a [sic] circular motions.

> "Sounds like someone is enjoying herself"

> Artemisa squirms against your hand, softly whimpering, "Maybe . . ."

> Inotep smirks and lets a finger slip inside you, at the same time, he leans forward and kisses you deeply.

> Artmisa's gasp is muffled by the kiss, and her nails dig in slightly into your arm.

> "That's not playing fair . . ."

> Inotep grins and withdraws his finger.

> "My apologies"

The dwarf, intrigued and amused, interrupts their encounter, albeit still within the parameters of role-playing:

> Gedran reveals his head from the shadows and begins to unzip his pantaloons.

> Gedran removes his Dwarven Hand Cannon and begins to stroke the barrel ever so slowly.

> Gedran lets out a quiet gasp as the cannon begins to expand in his hand.

> The couple's erotic moment disturbed, they do not respond well,

Artemisa growls menacingly at you.

Inotep growls, "You need to leave"

Playful, corporeal, if ultimately failed or thwarted, both of these examples show in different ways how erotic exchanges are potential forces waiting to be actualized, or, in Gedran's words, "expand." They show as well the creativity players use to push against the constraints of the intimacies tacitly and explicitly endorsed by the programmers of the game world.

In the dominant modes of *WoW* gameplay I describe—group and solo play—intimacy, and perhaps desire more generally, is both instrumental and linked to ideologies of success and failure. For scholars trained to think through intimacy and its institutions under late capitalism, this is familiar territory. Intimacy, again, is a set of normative ideals and aspirations tied to achieving capital and corporeal achievement; it is a central feature of the teleological life lived right. Intimacy in this way operates as one among other postmodern flows, fast and flexible with its deleterious but unavoidable effects on selfhood: alienation and anxiety, along with the sensual folding over of the commodity into experiences of interiority.[24] Even as intimacies in *Warcraft* depart from one key aspect of the metanarrative of intimacy, namely, the couple form and the child, they are still tied to other expressions of power, including the acquisition of goods and symbolic capital. This is normative intimacy minus the kids; the culpable self that employs intimacy as a means to an end.

In the encounters described above, however, we can begin to recuperate intimacy's virtuality, that is, its potential prior to capture, over or alongside its instrumentalization. Intimacy as playfulness, as friendship, or as sex is intimacy figured as a world-building project, something that might include instrumental iterations of desire but that also exceeds them. This is connectedness imagined as multiplicity or as multiverse where pleasure and consumption and production are folded into and over themselves and where emergent desires (whether from the past or the future) are nascent forces. In this modestly hopeful view of intimate virtualization, goal-oriented gameplay conditions but does not determine possibilities for creative engagement with the self and others.

The failure in each of these events to achieve understanding or to consummate an encounter should not be understood to represent closure. Rather, the gestures toward which these energies are oriented, propriety and eroticism alike, can be used to refigure intimacy as a means without end.[25] In this sense, then, intimacy is not what some have called "heternormative straight time" whose telos is successful coupledom and reproduction, but something characterized by gestures and interruptions, by a queer futurity or a "not-yet-here," in which nothing is necessarily being produced, only supported and endured.[26] What is being (queerly) supported and endured is, of course, desire itself, which rather than operating as something that merely produces a self through a series of successful achievements (understanding and consummation, or marriage and kids), allows selves to experience themselves as singularities that interface with other singularities, whether the singularity of the game world, or singular encounters with others.

For Deleuze, singularities are at once uniquely concrete and universal; they are universalized in themselves. As cultural critic Steven Shaviro puts it, "The singular directly touches the universal, without the mediation of any intervening terms."[27] What this might mean in *WoW* is that players, through their avatars and through face-to-face encounters, are shaped by the force of desire in concrete events and circumstances that index their particular histories, circumstances, and social locations—all that has come before. No other arrangement of desire, subject, time, space, event will yield the same result. In this way, singularities actualize an immanent or virtual capacity—they do not take any form, but only the forms they were potentially capable of, that they had a tendency to take. The virtual capacity of desire to *not follow* the general rules of a socially sanctioned form (coupled, straight, monogamous, "real") or particular teleology is a testament to the scope of tendencies intimacies are capable of. In *Warcraft,* then, intimacy's teleological endgame is interrupted insofar as the only progeny are fields of relations (whether instrumental or not) and the self itself, a convergence of pixilated image and enfleshed matter that endures and multiplies in its encounters with others as one avatar body among many in a multiverse as rich with potentiality as it is saturated by instrumentality.

CHAPTER THREE

Feeling Black and Blue

ONLINE GAY SEX PUBLICS AND BLACK AFFECTS

This used to be my Grindr profile (Fig. 3.1). Grindr is a smart phone app that brings gay cruising into the digital age.

This is a picture of me doing a twisted thigh stretch in Central Park. The image is heavily shadowed, but an interested viewer might note my lean muscly frame and the faint hint of tattoos on my back and shoulder. The text is simple: "Smart and easygoing yogi and professor usually living in upper Manhattan. Open to all sorts of real connections." Other identifying data appear in the upper left quadrant: my age (35), height (5'8"), weight (145lbs), and race (Mixed).

This assemblage of image, text, and facts emerges from a complex set of personal histories, dis-identifying and instrumental politics, and ambivalent structures of feeling. In my ordinary life, I'm not "Mixed." I'm variously black, interracial or both; I'm queer, gay, even more or less faggy. My Grindr profile reflects (I should say reflected, post-coupledom) a complex set of negotiations in which I ambivalently grappled with the racialization of desire and my own positioning in a hypercompetitive erotic marketplace in which whiteness enjoys preeminence.

Ten years after first logging on to the chat rooms at Gay.com, there's still something deeply mysterious to me about the significant part of my life that finds me dwelling in the queer space of the screen, and especially those virtual gay sex publics that have been my main entree into "the life." It's not only that my experiences resist as

FIGURE 3.1. A screenshot of one of my Grindr profiles.

much as they conform to particular discourses, whether psychoanalytically refracted longing or populist narratives of romance gone right (the serendipitous connection) or wrong (the excess of the hunt is addiction). It's that these spaces continue to affect me, to put me in motion, to infold new beginnings as much as repetition. That potential, or virtuality, is oriented toward a "not yet," a moreness that remains as much invitation as endless deferral. This chapter looks to some of the feelings of black men who navigate virtual sex publics, to the ways these feelings are organized in relationship to a range of injuries, minor and major. But, echoing the arguments I make elsewhere,[1] injury nestles alongside other feelings, including a vulnerability less certain than trauma, and the hard to pin down incipience that is an always already beginning, an ongoing process of becoming that I am calling optimism.

If vulnerability and incipience articulate a rather general set of affective orientations to online publics, how are these feelings articulated differently, or how do they matter differently for black gay men? And how might these feelings advance understandings of the relevance of black affects to social life for black folks and others? How might they further analyses of race beyond the representational paradigm that has dominated racial identity politics (a paradigm that has traditionally asked about how blackness looks in forms of popular culture, how it is numerically articulated in policies or statistical data, or even how its authenticity is obtained vis-à-vis racial performativity)? Here, I make some modest efforts to answer (or maybe only frame) these questions, using autoethnography and interviews with black men to examine feelings of racial anxiety, paranoia, and optimism in online gay sex publics. I try to add texture to black gay life by looking to these engagements with online spaces without settling on any one definition of what black queer life is or ought to be. I argue that feelings of anxiety and paranoia organize many of the processes and relations in these online queer spaces in ways that resemble prior and contemporaneous forms of racial injury, as well as emergent or ongoing forms of violence. Yet I also suggest that the promissory "not-yet-here"[2] of online spaces continues to make available transformative contacts and encounters, as well as precipitating a more expansive theoretical and political imagination.

Here, I draw on and contribute to several ongoing discussions about cyberspace, queers of color, and affect across the humanities and social sciences. The chapter confirms that rather than permit the transcendence of racial, gendered, or sexual difference promised by early cybertheorists,[3] online spaces reproduce and perhaps even heighten forms of racial injury, including ordinary microaggressions as well as overt or structural forms of racism.[4] And while no sustained engagement with cyberspace has emerged from the body of work called queer of color critique,[5] it adds to a number of black gay writers who have discussed the challenges of navigating virtual spaces.[6]

I draw on affect theory because it offers an important tool to look at the social significance of feelings in cultural life, and because it forms part of a capacious approach to matter and materiality, to life and politics. In a body of work concerned with "Public Feelings" located largely within feminist and queer studies, a diverse group of thinkers[7] have pointed to the ways that feelings, rather than belonging to intimate spheres of private life, are publicly circulating and structuring elements of our contemporary social, political, and economic worlds. Feelings are the language through which most of us express what is most significant in our lives, and they are sites from which to articulate a critical intelligence or activist practice differently.[8] This work has also explored racial archives of feelings, especially those related to memory, loss, and trauma.[9]

Affect theory represents an overlapping but distinct approach. Within a range of intellectual work inspired by Nietzsche, Bergson, Spinoza, Deleuze, and others, affect is tied to a vitalist turn in the humanities and social sciences that understands processual becomings and incitements to movement as constitutive of life itself. Affect theory represents a part of an approach that Nigel Thrift calls "non-representational theory."[10] In this work, affect is related to but distinct from emotions and feelings. As Eric Shouse parses these distinctions, feelings are personal and biographical, emotions are socially performed and circulating forms of feelings, and affects are pre-subjective or pre-personal "experience[s] of intensity."[11] This conceptualization of affect is especially important for the ways it identifies the capacity and power to put things into movement, to induce cascading and mutually intensifying changes.[12]

In what follows, I both retain and promiscuously mix these definitions. I do so because what I would call black affect likewise traverses various levels of analysis, as well as theoretical distinctions. Black affects put people and worlds in movement, and these affects are individually expressed, as well as socially performed and recognized.

Why only these three affective orientations? Anxiety, paranoia, and optimism are only three of many possible affects I might have chosen. And, after all, black folks have pioneered a vast range of affective styles and tonalities, including the blues, and also cool (even ice cold cool pace Eldridge Cleaver and Andre 3000), shade (SNAP!), funk, hope, killing rage, and R-E-S-P-E-C-T. The three affects I have chosen are, moreover, not what Phillip Fisher calls "vehement passions,"[13] but are more akin to moods or modes of attunement; I do not attend to anger or fear, or even to a more positive passion such as wonder. Instead, I have chosen three affective modes that have import for black life generally, that resonate with my own singular black queer life, and that unfold in compelling ways in the online spaces black gay men navigate.

FEELING BLACK AND BLUE

Black ontologies and epistemologies are deeply tied to a politics and poetics of feeling. Indeed, black people have often been figured as essentially feeling bodies and bodies that in turn hail more feelings to life: the angry black man or woman; nationalist or ordinary sincerity; disgust at the welfare queen; the crazy man (or woman);[14] longing for (black) self-help and uplift; post-traumatic slave syndrome; lusty Jezebels and Bucks; caring, warm mammy Oprah. As an intellectual genealogy of black and nonblack writers shows, black life and culture have been characterized by what Sianne Ngai calls "animatedness," an "excessively 'lively' or 'agitated'" performativity.[15] This emotional corporeality is moreover a central element to defining black racial authenticity. As Langston Hughes wrote of the "low-down folks" he looked toward to produce a new black artist, "Their joy runs, bang! into ecstasy. Their religion soars to a shout."[16] In his important book *Appropriating Blackness,* E. Patrick Johnson critiques Hughes's romantic elevation of black-working class people "as the site of racial authenticity."[17] Johnson observes that while "the pursuit of authenticity is inevitably an emotional and moral one,"[18] there is no essential fact of blackness. Rather, for Johnson blackness is defined in and through its appropriation (and contestations of its appropriation). The search for authenticity is infused with an emotional quality, and so are the "slippery" and ephemeral performative conditions that materialize racial blackness. These fleeting moments of authenticity demarcate who and what is included and excluded within the boundaries of blackness, as well as the "inexpressible yet undeniable . . . 'living in blackness'" that exceeds performative frameworks, what John L. Jackson Jr. has called "racial sincerity."[19] Authentic blackness, then, is recognized and constituted in and through feeling.

And part of what it is to feel black is to feel black and blue, to work through those forms of injury, real and perceived, that continue to shape black social worlds. From the historical and residual traumas of slavery to the persistent forms of de facto racism that limit opportunities for most black folk while criminalizing many others, suffering is part of what it means to be or to feel black. The "fracturing trauma" of race[20] includes the historical processes by which black people were systematically dehumanized for economic gain; the limits on spatial and class mobility; the persistent and dispiriting material effects of gaps in wealth; the ongoing reproduction of black people as commodities in which blackness circulates simultaneously as a form of cultural capital black people themselves rarely possess and as instrumentalized bodies that lubricate state, prison, and military bureaucratic and industrial complexes; and the psychological terrorism still waged against black people in the forms of overt antiblack racism as well as daily microaggressions enacted by a host of social actors, from white supremacists and liberals, to other ethnic minorities and black people ourselves. These material and immaterial injuries have obviously *affected* black life, and in turn put things into *movement(s)*. This inflow of injuries has evoked an affective call and response, from the "black mo'nin'"[21] that has given voice to social suffering and dreams of freedom, to proud and celebratory self-fashioning (Black Power, R-E-S-P-E-C-T), and fierce demands for recognition and redress. Black people have brought new feelings to life and made them available to broader publics.

In what follows, however, I take a less "meta" tack. I modestly story how I and some of the black gay men I've spoken to navigate online gay sex publics by looking to what are arguably effects or conditions of racial injury, anxiety and paranoia, as well as to the more spacious affective "openness" optimism invites, a moreness that points elsewhere than the differentiated specificity of hurt.

ANXIETY

In spite of the increasing tendency to understand anxiety as a psychological and physiological condition warranting therapeutic and/or pharmacological intervention, for my purposes here anxiety simply describes a state of heightened awareness, an arousal or agitation. Unlike paranoia, more on which below, it's not delusional. For the philosopher Martin Heidegger, anxiety is the ontological root and organizing mood of human life, a thrownness in which the "[authentic] self distinguishes itself from the world and becomes self aware."[22] Anxiety for Heidegger is structural, oriented toward indeterminacy; unlike fear, it has no object. Anxiety arises in ordinary circumstances in which "the world slips away, [and] we obtrude."[23] Though there are many important differences between these two frameworks, in Freudian psychoanalysis, anxiety is likewise conceived of as free-floating and without any particular object.[24] Sara Ahmed supports this basic assumption, but alters it to suggest that "anxiety tends to generate its objects, and to stick them together."[25]

Nearly all of the men I've spoken with over the last ten years agree that race matters in real and virtual spaces. Yet black men tend to express a more vigilant and apprehensive attention to this relevance. Vigilance and apprehension are of course familiar grooves for many black men whose lives and bodies are subject to a range of everyday and institutional pressures—gender normativity, surveillance, pathologization, hypersexualization—and reflect the ways anxiety is directed toward protecting against future harm. In the lives of black men anxiety operates as a "feeling of 'uneasy suspense,'"[26] an attunement to one's thrownness in larger worlds of disciplinary control and violence, as well as the powerful range of misreadings and misrecognitions that adhere to racist stereotypes in particular, and that in turn systematize this heightened awareness.[27] Focusing broadly on black anxiety, which of course affects women as well as men, and the sticky objects that it generates—money, family, health, home, the stuff of everyday life and everyday discrimination—is beyond the scope of this essay. Indeed, I cannot even focus on anxieties more specific to black gay life, such as HIV/AIDS. Instead, I look to a central practice of online life, profile creation.

In gay online sex publics anxiety structures the art of creating one's online representation. Men using these sites know that race matters because of the ways it is an essential element of the profile creation process. It is always a category included in key personal data (as even the minimal data in my Grindr profile above demonstrates) like age, weight, and height, and even dick size, and it is likewise one of the searchable criteria available for selecting partners. As legal scholar Russell Robinson notes, "Rather than simply passively permitting people to specify their racial preferences, some web sites demand that users identify their race and/or the races of the people they are willing to date. Such web sites thus require users who prefer not to state their race or other traits to provide information that others may then use to discriminate against them."[28]

At the outset, creating a profile arouses an attitude that is both reflective and forward-looking. Creating a profile forces one to attend to one's own desirability and to one's own desire, neither of which is self-evident, and both of which demand articulation in virtual spaces as much (perhaps even more) than in real ones. This is the mystery I gesture toward in my introduction: Who am I and what (or who) is it that I want? Sexuality, as the congeries of ideologies, histories, desires, identifications, and practices, is, as a number of queer theorists point out, deeply ambivalent, even incoherent. Simply creating a profile triggers an anxious response to "work[ing] out conflicting inclinations toward what kinds of closeness and distance we want, think we want, and can bear our object to have."[29] For black gay men, this creates a range of difficult choices, including those related to identity categories such as gay or queer, or articulating a relationship to the closet. This is accentuated by the ways in which, in a "gay marketplace of desire"[30] in which whiteness enjoys dominance, blackness generally possesses less value (more on which below), while at other times it achieves worth through fetishization. Thus, in this by no means exhaustive account, anxiety is anticipatory in the ways it is attuned to both visible and invisible sexualized and racialized patternings that, moreover, manifest differently in virtual spaces, and to rules that are not always evident but which we necessarily come to learn. Desire, identity, the closet, racism: anxiety accretes "like Velcro: it picks up objects that are proximate to it."[31]

In my still ongoing research with black gay men, a few relevant stories rise to the surface. Night, a young black gay man in his late twenties, embraced the obvious and not so obvious ways his blackness mattered in online spaces as a framing facticity:

> There's a section that doesn't want to hook up with you because you're black and a sect that does want to hook up with you because you're black. And for the sect that doesn't want to hook up with you cuz you're black, there's not a lot that you can do. I could change my personality, stay out of the sun, try to become Chelsea [the assimilated and homogenized gay "clone" found in New York's Chelsea neighborhood] or whatever, and I would be a very bad imitation of that. And I've seen people do that. And I'm like, okay that's not gonna work. Or I could over macho, hypersexualize myself as this Mandingo [the stereotyped hypersexual black male "Buck"] character that people are looking for. That doesn't really work for me either. Because I'm not that, I

guess, thug. I don't wear Timberlands and baggy pants and so . . . I know that there's a population that looks for that. So I don't really fit any of those two polarities when it comes to black gayness. I'm not trying to be Chelsea and trying to blend in and whitewash myself. Nor am I trying to hyper Africanize myself or ghettoize myself.

Night related this matter-of-factly, even emphatically. Yet his conviction also registers the anxiety of anticipation; he knew that his race would matter, so he wanted to make it matter obviously. And this steadfast positioning belies a deeper ambivalence. Betwixt and between, his assertion of an online (and offline) identity that resists the "polarities" of black gayness positioned him in opposition to certain conditions of black desirability that trade on stereotypes of the sexually insatiable and endowed Mandingo.

double consciousness

Another interviewee, Redy, a cultural activist and artist, describes that while he was conscious of his identity as a black man when he moved from Houston, a city with a large black population, to a predominantly white university town elsewhere in Texas, this consciousness didn't immediately extend to online spaces. He says of his early visits into online spaces that "[t]his was all happening in a predominantly white community in the South, so I didn't always feel like I understood the rules that had already been established because I was looking at it innocently and wasn't connecting the racial experiences that I observe in the real world." He initially used the online gay sites in this new city to search for the sorts of connections that had become familiar in his former home. This was not exactly a naive first effort, but it was one that didn't fully grasp what was going on, or what was at stake in this new milieu. Even as his dorm mate, "a gay big brother from hell," encouraged him to use the Internet to connect with guys—"Dude, go ahead and do it! Big Dicks!"—Redy increasingly came to learn that his racial and sexual identities as a "black power bottom" structured his ability to connect. His ability to hook up was sporadic—"There were so many people who were not into me! Not like [now in] New York, where I can get dick everyday. It really fucked with my psyche for a long time." Redy's online life in this whiter online world required him to become more anxiously attuned to the rules that governed these spaces, and to his own position within a racist economy of desire.

My own autoethnographic experiences likewise express an anxiety about how race comes to matter in these online spaces. In creating my own profile at chat-based sites such as Gay.com, or at cruising and hookup sites like Adam4Adam or Manhunt, I have often struck a politically ambivalent compromise. Increasingly, I tended not to select a definitive racial category that would disclose my political or physiognomic affinities to blackness in the portions of a profile that represent the most frequently searchable data fields. So rather than select Black/African American, I would typically select Mixed or Other. However, my apparent disavowal of a black identity was complicated by the ways I often included a more detailed account of my racial heritage, as in my profile at Dudesnude, where I say, "Mixed (black and white) if that matters." There's a story here, of course, or several. Briefly, when I first began using the Web site Gay.com for research and dating, the site only permitted users to select one racial identity category. At the time, I selected "mixed." Later, when it became possible to select multiple categories, I selected all that applied. Moments later, logged into the Austin chat room, I found myself engaged in a violently racialized dialogue with another user, whose chat began, "nigger, want to suck some dick?"[32]

This experience, along with the recognition that I could leverage my ambiguous racial presentation against pervasive antiblack racism, was what led me, at least in part, to the strategy I employed over the last few years. Yet my choice didn't necessarily reflect a rational approach to navigating these online worlds, but rather an experientially felt one, a hunch[33] that might equally be based in fantasy. My anxiety about committing to particular racial identifications and my subsequent ambivalence toward these identifications doesn't account for the ways users actually use racial information. Using just one relatively obvious example, my anxiety refracts a fantasy because it assumes users eliminate blacks as potential partners rather than conduct searches for their ideal white ones.

PARANOIA

"[T]he atmosphere in which we live, weighs upon every one with a 20,000-pound force, but do you feel it?"[34]

Paranoia, in its classic psychoanalytic interpretation, is at root oriented toward a queering of desire and bodies. In the case of Dr. Schreber,

Freud noted the ways his patient, who believed God was turning him into a woman, created a systemized and narcissistic narrative of a world in which he was the victimized center. While subsequent thinkers (notably Deleuze and Guattari) have challenged Freud's account, the original analysis is still compelling insofar as it offers a key axiom: paranoia is a project of worlding that indexes a social totality. Literary critic Sianne Ngai defines paranoia in broader terms, "not as mental illness but as a species of fear based on the dysphoric apprehension of a holistic and all-encompassing system."[35] In the United States and other global contexts, race is clearly one such social totality that conditions economic precarity, mobility, physical and psychic wellness, lifespan, and much more; yet charges of racism are frequently reduced to individualized complaints or failures, or to conspiratorial thinking.[36]

Contra Freud's account, in which the paranoid world is organized around the pathological experiences of an individual, John L. Jackson, in his recent book, *Racial Paranoia,* describes paranoia as an altogether more collectively experienced affect, generated in part by cultures of political correctness. In Jackson's account, racial paranoia is a pervasive speculative attention to hidden meanings and motives. For Jackson, the era of unabashed racism is over; however, while explicitly racist ideologies have been largely eliminated, they persist in historically salient ways (as debates about affirmative action or police brutality, to take two examples, show) as well as subtler ones that reflect our "racial present."[37] For Jackson, "our politically corrected present forces public expressions of racism to go underground."[38] This present is one in which racial thinking or racist attitudes materialize in minor instances that nonetheless demand interpretation. These interpretive practices seek out what he calls "de cardio racism," or racism of the heart. "Racial paranoia is [a] way of talking about . . . these repressed investments, sometimes irrational investments in race," and it "[is a way of] making sense of how people mine seemingly innocuous interactions for glimpses of what racial wolves in sheep's clothing might look like."[39]

In the context of the online gay sex publics I am preoccupied with here, the anxiety I describe above bleeds into something more than a heightened awareness. It bleeds into a paranoia that stories a world based on events and interactions that are clearly racialized, as well as those tantalizingly minor events Jackson describes that are interpreted as evidence of a worlded violence that positions the black gay man as a victim of invisible (perhaps especially in these online spaces) but pervasive forces. As my interlocutor Redy described above, he came to interpret his sporadic success in hooking up online as a function of his positioning in a white economy of desire. Another autoethnographic example serves as well. Throughout the summer of 2009, I used the Web site Manhunt to look for sexual and romantic connections. After nearly half a year, I'd met only three men, two of Asian descent, and one white. Indeed, the only one of these encounters that has endured as a friendship began when I noted and commented on Dil's explicitly antiracist profile text, where he wrote:

> I've noticed a lot of profiles claiming preferences like "only into whites, latinos, etc." or "no blacks and asians, no offense." I challenge you to imagine how this might be a form of racism, racial attractions ingrained in us through media images. Might your racialized desires be different if you grew up in a different society or time period? Consider this argument: we often ignore the ways institutionalized racism infiltrates our desires. We have in all of us these images of the muscular black top, or the submissive asian.

In a series of often-frustrated conversations with Dil and other friends, I engaged in an intense speculative analysis of why I wasn't able to find dates or tricks on Manhunt. Through deduction and intuition, I arrived at four possible answers: location (though I live in Manhattan, I live a considerable distance from the main gay ghettos of the city); timing (I was usually online and looking for connections during the morning and early afternoon rather than the evening or late at night); age (then at thirty-four, I'd crested the bell curve of gay male temporal desirability, i.e., eighteen to twenty-five, a belief I've subsequently discarded); and race (I experimented with different configurations, but always indicated, as I describe above, my racial difference). Of these four factors, I increasingly came to believe that race was the most salient, and I narrated this belief to my friends and recount it again here with the same conviction. Again, my analysis, like Redy's, belongs to the genres of minority epistemologies Harper calls "the evidence of felt intuition" and to Jackson's racial paranoia. Our "paranoia" indexes the ongoing imprinting of racialized microaggressions that produce powerful speculative fears about the effects racial difference can have not only on one's chances for getting laid but for more ontologically essential longings such as being wanted or loved.

floop

Of course, as the cliché goes, "just because you're paranoid doesn't mean they're not out to get you." In a recent study, UCLA law professor Russell Robinson demonstrated the ways black men were significantly disadvantaged in the erotic marketplace of Adam4Adam, a popular gay cruising site. In brief, he created profiles for white, Latino, Asian, and black tops and bottoms. He controlled for a range of variables, including appearance (all images were of the same light-skinned Latino man), and factors such as age, height, weight, musculature, and penis size. He found that the white and Latino men received similar numbers of messages, while the black and Asian men received significantly smaller numbers of responses. Black bottoms were what he calls "uniquely disadvantaged" in that they received the fewest responses of all (only four, compared to responses for whites and Latinos that ranged from the mid-twenties to mid-fifties). His third finding notes the ways that whites suffered no significant penalties regardless of the sex role they selected.[40]

For black gay men, going online in interracial environments to feel connected, or to more instrumentally look for dates or hookups, means grappling with a "species of fear" that indexes an antiblack world. Is it paranoia if it's true? Sianne Ngai answers affirmatively, suggesting that one can apprehend a total system from within without knowing that system's limits.[41] The boundaries of an antiblack world might, in other words, remain virtual (that is, immanent or imagined), yet one's paranoia is still a correct measure of and response to the weighty feeling of the twenty thousand pound racist atmosphere in which we live.

OPTIMISM

In this third section, I don't deny the affective atmosphere and impactful realities of hurt that black gay men negotiate online as elsewhere. Yet I also suggest that optimism and one of its attendant iterations, hope, offer up distinct but in some ways equally speculative orientations toward social worlds. Optimism is both an attunement to the not yet, and a queer perspectival shift toward or refraction of an interesting present. As Michael Snediker observes, optimism and hope tend to receive somewhat short shrift in many contexts, both elevated and vernacular.[42] That is, optimism is frequently figured as having "an allergic relation to knowledge"[43] and to be temporally inappropriate or premature. At the same time, there are renewed and earnest efforts to recuperate optimism and hope as crucially necessary modes of feelings as well as vital practices for intellectual or political engagement.[44]

In the context of my research, optimism indexes a commitment to "the open"[45] and, following Snediker and others such as Ngai, Thrift, and Anderson, a desire to nourish interest and the interesting, to broaden the scope of analysis (including the material as much as the "immaterial" realm of feelings) and, indeed, our repertoire of what is thinkable.

In spite of his consciousness of persistent antiblack racism in real and virtual spaces and homophobia in communities of color, Night, for example, refused to "cover"[46] his sexual desires for other men or his blackness: "I made a decision early on that I wasn't going to do the down low thing. Even at eighteen, nineteen, I thought that would be a bad idea." This decision led to a range of sexual encounters marked by race and racism, but not overdetermined by them. In one recollection, he laughingly referred to playfully disrupting the expectations of a white guy, who insistently wanted to meet—"Yo, yo, yo, what's up. Let's meet."—clearly looking for a big, black stud. But when Night went to meet the young man,

> I was wearing, like, slacks, and collared shirt, buttoned shirt, and I was like, oh, he's going to hate this—let's go!—because there's some weird screwy part of me that's like ooh, this person is looking for this [Mandingo], I'm gonna go do the exact opposite. And I came, and I approached him [here he affected a higher-pitched, "white" voice] and I was like, "Hello, how are—" and he was very, he was kinda like, he said like, "Oh, oh no" and looked at me, and I said, "It'll be good." And he said, "Really?" I was like, "*Yeah.*" And I put it in my mind to put in, to give, an outstanding performance. Which I did. Mainly. But it was like, part of me that was very strongly that was, like, to prove a point.

In his provocative intervention, "Black Optimism/Black Operations,"[47] Fred Moten refers to this interlocking of openness and refusal. Indeed, refusal can function as an opening, as a difference that calls other possible orientations into being, or at least highlights their immanence. Moten says, "Optimism always lives, which is to say escapes, in the assertion of a right to refuse, which is, as Gayatri Spivak says, the first right: an instantiation of a collective negative tendency to differ, to resist the regulative powers that resistance, that differing, calls into being."[48] Judith Halberstam has also recently emphasized the political potential of refusal, which she links to queer practices of failure. For Halberstam, failure can productively perform as a refusal of mastery. Losing and refusing can thereby work as counterdiscourses to winner-takes-all visions of success, social, political, sexual, or otherwise.[49]

In the story above, Night appears to have both differed from and conformed to expectations of black male sexual prowess. Yet his openness in regard to his own racial and sexual identities also enabled him to engage a fantasy of interracial sexual encounter with a critical and playful self-consciousness. Night also offers a more poignant example of optimism as an opening and refusal: at the time of our interview, Night had been celibate for two years, four months, and some change. There was no direct or inevitable link between his blackness or use of online spaces and his sexual sobriety (in fact, he continues to use the Web site OkCupid to go on dates with potential romantic partners). Rather, he has organized his past relationship to sex, which he now understands as compulsive, toward other, optimistic ends; he plans "to use sex for a higher purpose."

Redy described this laden refusal, a "negative tendency to differ," as similarly infused with a sense of futural optimism. He described occasionally getting sick of his online life and the "masks" he performed on sites like Adam4Adam because he didn't find what he was looking for, or he did, or, like me, he forgot what he was there for. When he gets really fed up, he said, "Then I delete my account. I don't want to be stale. I want to be *fresh*!" If Redy's attachment to being fresh registers, like Night's decision to be celibate, a desire for a more animated and animating not-yet-here, another story indexes the way optimism immanently lodges in an interesting present. Though Redy usually understands his online life as an instrumental search for sex, some of his encounters produced an infolded reflection, an incipient more only just discernible, and that suggested an immanent intimacy. This reflective attention emerged in one encounter with a white man he had only thought of as a trick, but who had a book that caught Redy's interest: "And so he had this book on his bedside table that had, that was about mourning partners who had passed away and that brought a sense of 'Huh, what's going on here?' I mean, I guess I had,

I guess I understood what I as looking for, I was looking for sex, like, in the moment, but that [book] gave me a whole 'nother context from where he was coming from." Redy's narrative of this ephemeral touch of something else and more index optimistic openings/refusals: it challenges the idea that the encounters that lead from online spaces diminish the possibility of feeling connected; it challenges the reduction of interracial sex to the hegemony of white libidinal economies; and it challenges as well both the operationalizing of intimacy as a trans-actional exchange, and the powerful demands that it not be. Together these refusals open and inspire a more spacious imagining of black gay life (or life more generally).

This is what Michael Snediker has recently described as a "queer optimism." Unlike most strands of optimistic thinking (including much of my own) that are linked (even if in unacknowledged or "mistraced" ways) to Leibniz and that are attached to a promissory future, queer optimism "doesn't ask that some future time make good on its own hopes. Rather, queer optimism asks that optimism, embedded in its own immanent present, might be *interesting*."[50] Such a cultivation of interests affirms extant and emergent black gay practices that lean toward "more than mere survival."[51] In spite of the "cramped worlds"[52] that many black gay men, like so many others, are forced to inhabit, we nonetheless creatively live lives that push inward and outward, that exceed the constraints of life as we know it: "There is hope that, in amongst the poisons of prejudice and general paranoia, some small beginnings can be made, summonings of what is not that can leap up and hear themselves, that are able to 'seek the true, the real where the merely factual disappears.'"[53]

At the very least, optimism suggests a broader repertoire of affec-tive possibilities than the violence and melancholy that my title, or the injuries that adhere to racial anxiety or paranoia, suggests. Here, I've used theories of affect to trace some of the ways the apprehensive vigilance black folk experience in ordinary life manifest more specifi-cally in the lives of black gay men who look for love and sex online. And I show how the affective capacities of black life are a good deal more expansive than fear or terror would appear to permit. Optimism in particular opens onto differences that are not merely the other side of power's insidious grasp. Instead, optimism opens onto, or moves into, spacious infolded presents and to alternative or emergent practices of "small beginnings" that help us to think about black feelings outside of the constraints of dialectics and toward a "more than representational" account of black queer life. Optimism builds worlds and it makes them livable. Feeling black and gay online hasn't therefore yet settled into cold facticity, but continues to shimmer with the right to refuse the certainty of no future, as an interesting interest in the present, or as "astonished contemplation" of the "not yet conscious."[54] Put another way, the persistent virtuality of online worlds keeps me hopeful and coming back for more, and this incipience simultaneously offers glimpses into a few of the ways black feelings matter materially not just in these online spaces but in many other lived sites of intimate social, political, or critical engagement.

CHAPTER FOUR

Justin Fucks the Future

Virtuality refers to the *connections that things are potentially capable of.* Virtuality is tendency, probability, latency.

—Arun Saldanha[1]

And it's always the same story.

—Kurt Eichenwald[2]

Our Nation's children are a precious gift and source of great hope for our future, and we have a responsibility to help them realize their full potential. In order to build a nurturing society that provides a safe, supportive environment for our young people, we must work together to combat the dangers that threaten their well-being. Internet predators and child pornography are profound evils that exploit children, shatter lives, and rob youth of their innocence.

—George W. Bush[3]

It's hard to be certain what former "camwhore" Justin Berry was looking for when he appeared on *Oprah* with his erstwhile savior, the then-esteemed *New York Times* journalist, Kurt Eichenwald. Was it to seek redemption? To warn parents about what their kids were doing with webcams? To tease and frighten viewers about the availability of kiddie porn? To lay claim to an expertise and entrepreneurial interest in victimhood and exploitation (and to a subsequent career path in technology consulting)? Certainly, taken together all of these affirm familiar narrative grooves, echoing what Eichenwald said in a CNN interview, with an admittedly different intent in mind, "it's always the same story."

Justin's story even more firmly implants an already widespread cautionary fable about the corruption of "erotic innocence," a notion explored by James Kincaid in two important works.[4] Kincaid examines the ways discourses about the sexuality of children operate simultaneously to disavow and reproduce children's erotic allure: "We make the child serve as the image both of what we desire and of what is altogether outside desire. But that is not our only dilemma. The erotic attraction to innocence is both forbidden (and thus, to some degree, forcibly repressed or at least denied) and so idealized as to be largely a fantasy attraction, cerebral lechery."[5]

Justin Berry's appearance on *Oprah* is part of a larger assemblage that illustrates some of the ways the figure of the Child orients so much of how we talk, think, and feel about virtual intimacies. Justin's story reminds us, in case we'd forgotten, that getting drawn into worlds of virtual relations often begins and ends in trouble. His story is magnetized to the dreams and dangers of technologically augmented childhood, and how technology exacerbates the gulf between technophilic youth and their technophobic parents who don't know the first thing about what their teens are really doing online. And it suggests that the bonds with our adolescent and teenage kids, already stretched thin by stresses of school, work, generational attitude, and hormones, are made yet more fragile.

There is, as well, pace Kincaid, the metacultural fascination with the sexual feelings and lives of these familiar yet increasingly distant creatures. Justin's story isn't unique, after all. Over the last several years, children themselves have become producers of child pornography, largely through "sexting," the practice of taking and sending sexually explicit images through ubiquitous digital technologies, usually cell phones.[6] His is one story among many, even if it achieves a particular traction through its invocation of techno(homo)phobia. Justin is one kid among others whose allure is heightened by going bad while trying to cling to his innocence; whose coming of age story evokes a sharp-edged nostalgia for our own sexual awakening; and whose failure and redemption (re-baptism and a career in public advocacy and consulting) mirror our own projects, or fantasies, of self-making.

Justin's story brings us into uncomfortably close contact with deep cultural desires and anxieties about childhood that are simultaneously materially real (in media forms and cultural fantasies about the erotic innocence of children), concrete (in actual molestation, neglect, and abuse), and virtual (in profligate, immanent, latent speculations on the possibilities for intergenerational sex). If virtual intimacy refers, in part, to commonsensical notions about what new technologies are doing to our forms of relating, especially bad things, it is this powerful and powerfully laden figurative Child that explicitly and implicitly frames many of these beliefs.

Who is this capital "C" Child I am suggesting is central to debates about virtual intimacies? By Child, I'm not so much referring to the actual, more or less adorable, stinky, curious, beloved, playful, thoughtful, rebellious, anarchic daughters, sons, nieces, nephews, or strangers we encounter in our ordinary lives as to the collectively assembled and very potent figure of The Child, which we've charged with ultimate affective and political significances: innocence, delight, pleasure, hope, even evil, as well as, as I discuss below, the burden and the promise of "the future."

Here, I outline Justin Berry's story as the story of this structuring Child, and I focus especially on the ways this figure affects understandings of the structure of and future for virtual intimacies. In particular, I focus on how, on the one hand, the anxieties and images that accrete to and emanate from the erotically innocent Child provoke and reinforce cultural anxieties and fascination with children's sexuality. On the other hand, I track the ways anxieties materialize in a range of discursive, political, and legal effects that do little to protect children. Rather, these effects tend to erode the rights of children and adults alike, especially those rights related to privacy and freedom from government and corporate intrusion. And for the purposes of my larger arguments about virtual intimacies, the force of this figure of the Child and his story of lost innocence highlights a key paradox in our attitudes about virtual intimacies: the virtual offers a means to realize our aspirations to connect, while our anxieties about the corruption of erotic innocents make our aspirations and connections alike irredeemable. Along the way, I disrupt the coherence of the story Berry and Eichenwald tell Oprah. My goal here is to unpack a bit of this story in an effort to understand how the volatile mixture of imagined notions of childhood, sex, and technology shape so much of the talk about and efforts to mediate virtual intimacies.

First, though, the Child.

NO FUTURE

In his important polemic *No Future,* Lee Edelmen engages in a ferocious critique of what he calls "reproductive futurism," an ideology that depends on and reproduces the figure of the child as the basis on which political hopefulness and the rhetorics that articulate it depend.[7] Reproductive futurism goes further than hetero- or homonormativities in its deployment of the Child. Children in the latter are effects, procreative sums of an intimate life lived right, that is, usually monogamous and committed and, ideally, located in a stable social and economic context. Children here are invariably success stories, a measure of completion or arrival, and they are innocents who will need to be socialized and educated. They are, of course, also miracles to which we (must) bear witness. Above all, in a culture of ambient fear, they appear as potential victims who need anticipatory protection from practically all fronts: natural and social environments, schools, other kids, and caretakers, including parents themselves.[8] Yet Edelman's reproductive futurism goes farther than this notion of childhood endorsed by normative ideologies and institutions of intimacy. In Edelman, the figure of the Child becomes a central organizing figure of the Symbolic order writ large, crystallized in the notion that that "the children are our future." Language, affect, and politics are all likewise routed through the circuit of the Child, and its invocation is a variously earnest, banal, cynical, yet utterly requisite gesture of obeisance to sentimentality, to a virtual Child operating as a cultural reservoir for hopefulness and longing. Turning to this Child, though, is also a disavowal of our own immediate and imminent culpability; it is a failure to imagine and to take responsibility for a future in which we might continue to function as important social actors. This is not Edelman's argument, however. He doesn't offer a political escape route, or reason for hopefulness. Rather, he insistently identifies the ways "the fantasy subtending the image of the Child invariably shapes the logic within which the political itself must be thought."[9]

While Edelman's condemnations cast a broad net, he takes queer politics especially to task for relying on this same reproductive futurism that "impose[s] an ideological limit on political discourse . . . casting outside the political domain, the queer resistance to this organizing principle [the Child] of communal relations."[10] He argues instead that a queer politics should be constituted by an embracing of the negative, a rejection of reproductive futurism, the child, even politics altogether.

The ethical project of queerness, as Edelman articulates it, then, is of negation in service of a more vital and unencumbered jouissance. So, he says, "fuck the social order and the Child in whose name we're collectively terrorized."[11] Fuck the Child, and fuck the future.

Child and future fucking are precisely what appear to be at stake in Justin's story, though perhaps not entirely in the ways Edelman might argue.

INNOCENCE LOST

At first glance, Berry's story appears relatively straightforward. A teenager buys a webcam so that he can "meet girls his own age," but something goes wrong and he's drawn into a "sordid online world" where men pay him in gifts and cash to perform in front of the camera; there's an evolution, or devolution rather, in which he goes from taking off his shirt to having sex with Mexican prostitutes and recruiting minors to appear in videos with him.[12] At least this is how things were initially framed in Kurt Eichenwald's *New York Times* story that brought Berry to the attention of the larger public and reignited the always latent collective fretting and fantasizing about kiddie porn. Here's a sketch of the original *Times* story.[13] While investigating money laundering, respected journalist Kurt Eichenwald accidentally comes across what appears to be a connection between a porn star and an Internet fraud case.[14] He follows the lead and along the way discovers that the adult star isn't an adult at all, but a child, albeit one on the threshold of his majority. Further digging leads Eichenwald to discover a network of "camwhores," people who exchange sexually explicit webcam performances for money, child pornographers and pedophiles. It's these sophisticated and tech savvy pervs who seduced and then exploited Justin Berry, a good kid with a bit of a troubled home life and a techie streak that hurt more than helped him. Berry's corruption began when he accepted gifts from men who approached him online after he'd set up his webcam account he'd hoped would help him feel more connected. Although these men praised him and gave him presents, soon they asked him to do other things, like taking off his shirt, his boxers, masturbating. In Eichenwald's words,

> So began the secret life of a teenager who was lured into selling images of his body on the Internet over the course of five years. From the seduction that began that day, this

soccer-playing honor roll student was drawn into performing in front of the webcam—undressing, showering, masturbating and even having sex—for an audience of more
than 1,500 people who paid him, over the years, hundreds
of thousands of dollars.[15]

With the help of some of his fans, Justin Berry sets up Web
sites that feature him and other boys, and later girls and women,
engaged in sex acts. This goes on for five years, and, as Eichenwald
notes, he earns hundreds of thousands of dollars; indeed, at perhaps
the most lucrative period of his camwhore career, his estranged father
helps him out with the business in Mexico, where Justin's father had
absconded after charges of insurance fraud. After he enters the age of
majority, Berry has himself begun to recruit minors and this is about
the time when the journalist becomes involved. Eichenwald, acting as
both Good Samaritan and hardcore activist journalist, gets the kid to
"flip"; Berry gives Eichenwald access to this sick world with children
in imminent danger, Eichenwald gets Berry to agree to get off drugs
and shut down the Web sites, and helps him get an immunity deal so
together they can put the predators and pedophiles away. The story
is a hit, spawning several spinoffs, media appearances, and not a small
bit of controversy (much more on which below).

This is my gloss anyway, but Oprah puts it best in her promo for
Berry's appearance on her program, her dramatic voiceover cut with
scenes from her interview and on-screen text:

An honor student, class president is risking his life to be here

Death threats, who's making them?

How this boy became an Internet porn star

*The first time you were asked to take off your pants, what did
you think?*

This could be your child

*How many different occasions were you molested ("So many I
can't even count")*

The little gadget that made it all possible

We'll show you just how easy it happens[16]

As if we needed reminding, Berry's story jerks our attention to a particular set of dangers—online predators violating boyhood innocence, a dis-integrating Web that offers the promise of easy money but only at the cost of that innocence. These are the explicit dangers, yet others lurk below the surface, marked by what Susie Bright calls a "homophobic *ick* factor": gay predators in particular are figured as especially adept at derailing an otherwise good boy off the proper developmental track toward heterosexuality; and technology can abet this sexual ambivalence.[17]

Yet Eichenwald offers the public a way out. That is, this is a story not just of innocence lost, but of redemption. In Eichenwald's account, Berry gets off drugs, the men most intimately involved with his exploitation are arrested (the original *Times* article ends with Berry helping law enforcement catch one of his molesters), laws are enacted, task forces created, and parents are empowered with the knowledge of what a webcam can do and what they should do with it—throw it away. If this story seems familiar, it's because it is, bringing together fears about kids and sex with our fears of technology.

I've already noted the *Times* and Oprah, but the story has had wider cultural traction. On a CNN spot, Berry's story is sandwiched between stories about an epidemic of turkey-frying fires, rape, and murder.[18] After warning us that viewers won't want young kids to watch the story (so they won't be traumatized, or so they won't get any ideas?), a short video clip of Berry appears telling parents to throw their kids' webcams away. An unidentified man asks, "Why?" and Berry responds, "Because you are letting the pedophiles into your kids' bedrooms." Eichenwald joins the reporter live to talk about how pedophiles groom kids by convincing them that their online friends are the only friends that count. He also talks about the money.

The money is important, though it's not always clear why. Is it because of the amount of money (hundreds of thousands of dollars)? Because Justin was so good at getting it? Are we meant to be shocked by the money pedophiles are willing to spend or shamed that we aren't as industrious? But Eichenwald notes that not all kids become camwhores for the money. They do it, he says, for attention. What he can't imagine, of course, is that the camwhores themselves might have a range of emotional and erotic investments for performing online other than needing love and attention from the surrogate predator parents, such as sexual pleasure.

NPR's *All Things Considered* also reports on the *New York Times* investigation: "The booming business of child pornography that's transmitted over the Internet with web cams. These are minors using web cameras in their own paid pornography sites. Hundreds of them." Most of the report is devoted to Eichenwald's success in saving Berry and dealing a blow to this child porn industry. Here, Eichenwald notes that he's "delighted that the industry has been massively disrupted" and provides listeners with a remedial guide to how the business operates: "There are such things called portals—what those are are central websites that list where the teen websites are located . . . at least every large portal that was associated with Justin has been shut down. Somebody compared it to turning the lights on in the kitchen when the cockroaches are all in the center and they have scattered."[19] The problem, however, is that Eichenwald's and the *Times*'s efforts represent only a temporary fix. The pornographers will be back because "there's an enormous amount of money to be made in this business." The solution? Well, that's clear. He says, "Really what it comes down to is the parents. Justin said it very well in one of my interviews with him. When I asked him what parents should do, he said, 'take the webcams and throw them in the garbage.' . . . The only thing that is going to stop this is good parenting."

Berry's story even made it Down Under. The episode of the Australian version of *60 Minutes* that tackles online sexual predation is especially hyperbolic. The exposé, "Web of Evil," gives audiences "a very rare opportunity to hear firsthand how these men stalk, entrap and seduce their young victims. And even more importantly, how to keep your own kids safe."[20] This story features Berry back at his California home, reflecting on all the bad things that happened there (though it was mostly him alone in his room—he had another apartment to run the business out of), and a profile of an FBI task force agent who tells the host a story so graphic it has to be edited out. The journalist finds it impossible to imagine that men will do these terrible things to kids and almost as hard to contemplate having to look at this stuff in order to stop it from happening. He's grateful too, though, that someone's doing it.

None of these stories question the relationship between sexual abuse and online predators. Viewers are informed that online child pornography is a booming twenty billion dollar industry and that it is the anonymity of the Net that affords predators such easy access to kids. And the implication is that most of the sexual exploitation of children is happening online. All of these claims are patently false. But a National Center for Missing and Exploited Children (NCMEC) fact sheet at first appears to substantiate them; it provides these alarming statistics about online youth victimization:

> Approximately one in seven youth online (10 to 17-years-old) received a sexual solicitation or approach over the Internet.
>
> Four percent (4%) received an aggressive sexual solicitation—a solicitor who asked to meet them somewhere; called them on the telephone; or sent them offline mail, money, or gifts.
>
> Thirty-four percent (34%) had an unwanted exposure to sexual material—pictures of naked people or people having sex.
>
> Twenty-seven percent (27%) of the youth who encountered unwanted sexual material told a parent or guardian. If the encounter was defined as distressing—episodes that made them feel very or extremely upset or afraid—forty-two percent (42%) told a parent or guardian.[21]

I'll return to these statistics in a moment, but first I want to focus on some of the controversies the Berry story generated.

The certainty that there is reason for alarm—that is, the almost commonsensical belief that online child porn and predation is an already large and ever-growing problem—goes largely unexamined, but a few critics did raise questions about the story, largely centering on Eichenwald's reporting methods. At first, these questions centered on his blurring of the lines between journalism and advocacy, especially in assisting Berry to get an immunity deal.[22] Later, more questions were raised, mostly in the Left alternative press by Debbie Nathan, after court proceedings against one of the men accused of molesting Berry revealed that Eichenwald had paid Berry two thousand dollars to gain initial access to him (Berry was auctioning an in-person meeting to the highest bidder, and Eichenwald won). Later, the *Times* appended this fact to the story (the auction remained unmentioned, though), and a public editor raised some questions about Eichenwald's and his editors' actions.[23] But because the money had been repaid before the story was written, it was concluded that the underlying integrity of the reporting remained uncompromised. Debbie Nathan, writing in *Salon* and *Counterpunch,* however, offered a persistent and stinging critique of Eichenwald, the *Times,* and the uncritical acceptance of widely circulating but misunderstood, misrepresented, or simply false claims about the dangers kids face online.

In her first *Salon* story, which *Salon* censored after complaints from Eichenwald, Nathan was sympathetic to Eichenwald's story even as she skeptically examined his methods. Her article, "Why I Need to See Child Porn," questioned why Eichenwald was able to look at child porn for his story while no other reporters or researchers were likewise permitted.[24] She describes her own anxiety after stumbling across child porn while researching a book project and realizing that simply by visiting the site, accidentally or not, she was now subject to prosecution: "Technically, according to federal statutes, just visiting a kiddie-porn site makes you a lawbreaker, because regardless of why you went there, the images end up in your hard drive. You 'possess' child porn, which is a serious crime. You can notify the authorities. You can clean up your cookies and your cache. Still, you broke the law. The feds might excuse you, or they could arrest you. It's entirely up to them."[25] She also cites the case of Lawrence Matthews, a former NPR journalist arrested, tried, and convicted of possessing child porn, who claimed he was researching the sites for a story he was work-ing on (his previous stories on child porn aired on Washington radio and appeared in the *Washington Post*). Essentially, independent studies of the prevalence of child pornography are prohibited.[26] Nathan does cite Philip Jenkins, who managed to partly sidestep this prohibition by disabling the downloading of images on his computer and simply reading the text that pedophiles wrote on their sites. His research contradicted some government claims (such as the scale of the online child porn problem), while confirming others (it's a real problem), and made the argument that legitimate researchers needed access to these data to better fight against Internet-mediated child exploitation.[27]

Clearly, then, Nathan argues, Eichenwald must have himself bro-ken the law in researching the story, since to simply look at child pornography is a crime. He claims he (and/or the *New York Times*) looked at more than two hundred sites, including Berry's. From my own reading as well, it appears his detailed descriptions of the images also suggest that he was talking about images he'd personally seen. In one of the more lurid descriptions, he says, for example, "In the photograph, the model is shown rising out of a bubble bath, suds dripping from her body. Her tight panties and skimpy top are soaked and revealing. She gazes at the viewer, her face showing a wisp of a smile that seems to have been coaxed from off-camera."[28] After Eichenwald and the *Times* threatened to sue for libel, *Salon* removed the article and issued an apology, citing a provision to US Code § 2252 (a provision that, not incidentally, hadn't helped Matthews) that enabled the *Times* and Eichenwald to research the story. In a more vindictively personal note to Nathan, Eichenwald wrote, "Salon has elected to remove this piece of garbage from their site. However, if you should attempt to mischaracterize and misrepresent my actions again, in any other forum, let me assure you, I will take immediate and decisive legal action against you. And under no circumstances will I settle until you are financially wiped off the face of the earth. People like you are the maggots of journalism; you are everything that is wrong with this profession. Clear enough?"[29]

Nathan's queries, though, are serious ones, and the provision the *Times* cites simply does not do what the newspaper claims it does. As Nathan explains in an interview with sex educator and cultural critic Susie Bright, the provision cited only applies if one has fewer than three images and, more importantly, the provision is only an affirmative defense, that is, one only uses it after one has already been arrested for child pornography. It does not apply to any willful effort to find child porn for any purposes.[30]

So, if the careful study of online child porn by journalists and academics is prohibited (excepting Eichenwald's and Jenkins's clever roundabout research), where do the twenty billion dollar estimate or the statistics published on the NCME page come from? The truth is that even obtaining reasonable estimates for legal pornography can prove difficult; in 2001 journalist Dan Ackman famously debunked some of the then most widely circulating numbers that put the industry at between ten and fourteen billion dollars. Rather, he argued, drawing on limited available data, the numbers were significantly less, and a generous estimate would place the adult industries' total revenues at less than four billion, although these numbers have likely risen over the last ten years. And while the numbers on the NCME fact sheet are accurate, these facts do not offer clear strategies for interpretation or application. David Finkelhor, for example, a leading child victimization researcher, whose data provides a basis for the fact sheet, suggests a willingness to discuss sex among adolescents, including talking to teens about sex, might do more to curb online victimization than media or political hysteria.

Yet within the widespread context of aroused agitation surrounding the Berry case, no one challenged the underlying claims except Nathan, who, during the 1980s and '90s gained prominence (and no small measure of contempt) for challenging narratives of child sexual abuse, especially of the epidemic Satanic sort folks were saying were happening at daycares around the nation.[31] So, in spite of Eichenwald's threat to sue her and *Salon*'s unwillingness to contest the notion that US Code § 2252 exempted the *Times* from the child porn statutes, Nathan doggedly continued her reporting for other magazines, including *Counterpunch,* where she offers the only sustained critique of Berry's own narrative. At this point, court cases against four men associated with Berry's case (accused of either facilitating the business end of things or molesting him) are proceeding, and Berry's story has had its fifteen minutes, with him emerging as a victim and a hero. Nathan, though, carefully follows the trials and reviews the court transcripts; and while remaining sensitive to the larger contexts of abuse and exploitation, she also paints an altogether more complex portrait of Berry, one in which he emerges as less an innocent straight boy corrupted by tech savvy queer predators than as an equally tech savvy, ambitious, sexually flexible, self-interested, and even cynical entrepreneur.

Nathan's research includes several salient points: Berry, far from being the straight boy who'd been derailed by the flattery and largess of pederasts, demonstrated an altogether looser sexual identity. His first sexual experience at thirteen was not simply molestation at the hands of Gino Tunno (who was already serving a sentence for sexual abuse of a child while the other Berry cases developed), but a threesome that involved Tunno, Berry, and another teen, "Vic," a friend of Berry's, who had his own camwhore business and with whom Berry sometimes performed. While Eichenwald and Berry suggest that Ken Gourlay was the first to molest Berry, it's clear that Gourlay didn't meet Berry until much later. The sexual contact that convicted him happened when Berry was two months shy of his sixteenth birthday. Another: It's very unlikely that Justin went to Mexico simply at the invitation of his father, as Eichenwald suggests. Rather, at sixteen, Justin, in spite of his bravado, feared he was already under investigation by law enforcement. He fled because he thought the law was moving in. As Nathan writes, "It's not clear which crimes he was worried about. In addition to producing and distributing child porn, he was also involved in credit card theft, sitting in his apartment with at least a dozen numbers he'd purloined from the Internet, using them to order $5000 worth of merchandise."[32] Perhaps most damning (certainly for Eichenwald) is evidence that challenges the timeline of Berry's departure from the business. It appears that the monies Eichenwald sent were used by Berry to add new content to his essentially dead Web site—that is, he recruited and paid at least one new minor to appear after he'd flipped for Eichenwald.

Above all, Nathan adamantly refuses Berry the redemption guaranteed by others.

One way of putting this is to say that she refuses Berry's virtualization as Edelman's Symbolic Child. By beginning from the perspective that Berry must be an innocent victim, because no thirteen-year-old boy would, without the expert manipulation of pedophiles, be willing to display himself online, have sexual relationships with older men, or recruit other minors into the camwhore biz, most media stories about him abstract the concrete Justin Berry into the Child who holds in tension a congeries of fears and anxieties about the sexual lives and feelings (and especially queer ones), technological literacy, vulnerability, and wildness of youth. Unlike the more expansive philosophical constructions of the virtual—as potential, probability, latency—the virtual Child forecloses possibility. The only potential it permits is enforced: the immanent potential of victimization and endless, but fettered, innocence. In its encounters with sex, technology, or the collision of the two, the Virtual Child enforces a habitual contraction, closing off lines of flight that might interrogate the risks and dangers, or pleasures and encounters, it lays constitutive claim to. Or, more concretely, it operates to make challenges like those Nathan poses—challenges to its underlying virtuality—appear shrill, dangerous, and crazy. After all, who doesn't want to protect kids from predators?

To refuse the Child its virtuality is, in turn, to refuse it redemption.

To talk about the Virtual Child in this way is not to deny the existence of some very real effects it engenders (or the fact that real kids are neglected, exploited, hungry, etc. in ways far more widespread than the threat of online predators). The real effects include further deepening the narrative grooves about erotic innocence that form part of the larger discourse of reproductive futurism: the Child to whom we submit not just our future but our present insofar as politics, pleasure, and social life more generally are and must be framed in the Child's service.

These effects are buttressed by statistics like those I cite above, or the widely touted but entirely unsupported claim about the monetary scale of the child porn industry. Closer examination of the statistics reveal that some of the sexual solicitation occurring online happens between kids and, indeed, that the definition of sexual solicitation is itself quite wobbly—it refers to any talk about sex, not necessarily a demand to have it. To take a specific example, Ad Council service ads in 2005 reported that one in five children were solicited online, a misleading use of data that was then already five years old and that referred only to children who spent time online. Of the 20 percent who received an online solicitation, only 3 percent reported aggressive solicitation.[33] A second, more recent survey conducted in 2005, found, among other things, that while more youth were exposed to unwanted sexual material online (that is, material they did not actively seek out) and online harassment, fewer were the object of unwanted sexual solicitation.[34]

As for child porn being a twenty billion dollar industry, this is, as far as I can tell, an entirely imaginary number that gained credence only through its repetition. Carl Bialik, the *Wall Street Journal's* "Numbers Guy," tried to track down the original source of this number, as did freelance writer Daniel Radosh, and both reached run arounds and dead ends; the number had variously been attributed to a consulting firm and the FBI, though neither took credit for it in the end.[35] Indeed, as the well-known *Forbes* article from 2001 outlined, determining the scale of the legal porn industry is difficult enough and depends in part on whether one focuses only on commercial pornography or on the larger sex industry.[36]

For the most part, the fears about kids and the Web have resulted in a range of efforts to expand regulation and surveillance of online life through laws, committees, and task forces. While examining juridical effects in detail isn't my aim here, there are five laws that have particular bearing on children and the Internet.

In 1998, Congress enacted the Children's Online Privacy Protection Act (COPPA). In spite of loopholes and widespread corporate noncompliance, this is the only law designed to protect children from the most invested and capacious online predators: corporations. COPPA grants the federal government the ability to limit the sorts of information companies can collect about children under thirteen years of age. Also, in the late '90s, Congress passed two other Acts: The Child Pornography Prevention Act (CPPA), which was intended to broaden the ban of child porn to include virtual depictions (including computer-manipulated imagery and pictures), and the Child Online Protection Act (COPA). Then, at the turn of the millennium, Congress also passed the Children's Internet Protection Act (CIPA) and the Neighborhood Children's Internet Protection Act (N-CIPA). The last two laws tie government funding to schools and libraries to the implementation of censorship and surveillance software.

In an article about children and technology that interrogates practices and ideologies of surveillance and censorship, researcher Gregory Donovan outlines the ways most legislation, excepting COPPA, that purports to protect children functions in effect quite differently, performing work in the public imagination—easing our minds that the government is looking out for kids—but largely benefiting a range of corporate and institutional efforts to constrain the freedoms available online, especially those afforded by anonymity.[37] In fact, most of the post-COPPA legislation erodes privacy protections for children and citizens alike in the service of creating a semantic Web, a reformatted cyberspace in which data is automatically collected and interpreted (social networking sites and Google are the collectors and interpreters par excellence). Donovan argues in part, then, that fears about children's online sexuality have enabled private corporations to be granted powers of public surveillance and censorship while government powers are increasingly soliciting private data.[38]

Some of the laws purporting to help kids have struggled to achieve legal credibility. CPPA, which tried to criminalize virtual images, for example, was struck down for being overly broad and violating free speech. COPA has been deemed unconstitutional and cannot be enforced. The law, which sought to limit youth access to any "harmful" material, including but going beyond obscenity, was deemed in violation of the First and Fifth Amendments in multiple court rulings. One moment in its litigation history is especially relevant. In *Ashcroft v the ACLU*, the Department of Justice issued subpoenas to search engines to gather data about the sorts of Web searches users conducted. Most search engines complied, although Google successfully fought to limit the information it provided. While the court ultimately ruled in favor of the ACLU, and has refused to hear subsequent appeals, thereby maintaining the injunction against COPA's enforcement, the DOJ's relative ease in acquiring private data represented yet another significant blow to privacy protections in the wake of the War on Terror.

If laws that venture too far into the muddy definitions of U.S. obscenity law have met with limited success, ones that bring together censorship and surveillance in order to protect children have been considerably more actionable. CIPA and N-CIPA remain disturbingly intact and essentially guarantee that public schools and libraries, especially those most dependent on federal funding, must install censorship and surveillance software. CIPA includes this very broad language about what constitutes an Internet safety policy: "An Internet safety policy must include technology protection measures to block or filter Internet access to pictures that are: (a) obscene, (b) child pornography, or (c) harmful to minors (for computers that are accessed by minors)." More recently the as yet unenacted Deleting Online Predators Act (DOPA) bill, which emerged in the wake of Berry's case, would build on CIPA to prohibit youth access to social networking sites and chat rooms in institutions that receive E-rate funding.

In addition to these federal bills, then-attorney general Alberto Gonzales initiated Project Safe Childhood (PSC) in mid-2006. Gonzales offered his first comments about this initiative, which provides funding and coordination, a few days after Berry testified before Congress. While Berry is not directly mentioned by Gonzales in his comments about PSC or the documents themselves, it's clear that it's Berry and others like him who form part of the impetus for the initiative. Indeed, Gonzales's extremely aggressive if relatively short-lived efforts to not only focus on online sexual predation of kids but to prosecute obscenity cases was contingent on the more than two thousandfold increase in investigations and arrests connected to the production and distribution of child porn. Other than the explosion of convictions, which have in turn required more and more people to register in publicly accessible sex offender Web sites, perhaps the most visible result of this initiative was a series of public service announcements that aired in 2008. Focused largely on discouraging teens from talking to strangers online and publishing their personal information, they also addressed the rising phenomenon of cyberbullying.

Laws, taskforces, and PSAs are all artifacts that represent an ambivalent sort of concretization of the fears that swarm around children's online sociality. Indeed, some of the foremost experts on online youth victimization and socialization expressed concern about the motivations and efficacy of legislative and outreach efforts. Being good empiricists, they suggest that laws be enacted only once there's good data—it's no good just to follow a hunch or to let parental feelings of being over-whelmed drive the implementation of legal restraints to youth access. In a panel discussion sponsored by the Congressional Internet Caucus Advisory Committee (CICAC), two of the most prominent researchers of online youth victimization, David Finkelhor and Michelle Ybarra, not only correct some common misunderstandings about the research that exists, but suggest that existing efforts might be insufficient and that intensive interventions might better limit the risk of some chil-dren and adolescents to become victims of online harassment or sexual predation.[39]

These levelheaded researchers try to do the good academic work of putting things into context. Indeed, in the discussion, Ybarra asks important foundational questions: "Is it the Internet that increases the risk of kids or is it kids that are increasing their risk? So is it the Internet that's causing victimization or is it these life situations, these characteristics that kids have? And what if instead of trying to address the internet, we try and address the kid?" Together, Finkelhor and Ybarra seem to urge prudence and suggest there might be good reason to slow some of the hysteria about kids' online activities. Yes, there are real problems they say, but all in all kids seem to be doing pretty well. For example, most of the kids who find disturbing stuff online talk to their parents about it. Certainly these academics challenge some of the more conservative beliefs about childhood sexuality, admitting that young people might not only be unwilling victims of virtually mediated sex; they might themselves be seeking this information out, a point confirmed by Ybarra. The Internet, they admit, does operate as a key, and even valuable, medium through which children express their curiosity about sex and experiment with their developing sexual identities.

If all this sounds a great deal less hyperbolic, it's because it mostly is. Ybarra and Finkelhor each call into question the current outreach methods. Ybarra notes that while public service announcements might be good for reducing stigma (about what exactly, though—cyberbul-lying or the shame associated with connecting online?), they don't really do intensive interventions in these kids' lives. Ybarra suggests the best use of monies would be to fund interventions for the highest risk kids. If Ybarra's suggestion sounds reasonable, and I think it probably is, Finkelhor's seemingly contradictory claim also makes sense. For Finkelhor, it's important to use messaging for teens that affects them. So, he suggests, it might make sense to employ shame in order to reduce youth's risky online behavior: "So for example, we have to educate them about why hooking up with a 32-year-old guy has major drawbacks to it like jail, bad press, public embarrassment."

Of course, Kincaid would say that these sorts of reasonable assertions, or the actions that might result from them, would deprive us of the pleasure we take in talking about the sexual risks and dangers our innocently erotic children experience.

As well, reading through the transcript of this panel discussion, I'm struck by the way certain concepts remain fixed, especially risk and victimization. So while the details matter—to better understand what's a problem and what isn't—the underlying belief is that kids still need help navigating their online lives. One example Finkelhor offers at first appears to be an even more complex and troubling portrait. He describes a "typical case" of a thirteen-year-old girl who has multiple sexual experiences with someone she meets online, who describes feelings of love, and who resists efforts to prosecute him. This disruption in our expectations is smoothed over, though, by her age. Of course, no thirteen-year-old could be trusted to make good decisions about sex. But what if she were fifteen, sixteen, seventeen? And how does the use of this generically obvious victim reflect on our own early sexual experiences?

I think it pretty likely that kids need support and direction from attentive parents in helping them navigate sociality, and certainly love and sex, in their offline as much as their online lives. But it seems that part of our efforts—legislative, therapeutic, academic—go farther than helping them to make more mature decisions. It looks more as if we need to redeem their erotic innocence, and tell the story of their redemption in the process.

REDEMPTION

Perhaps academics are disinclined to give redemption its due. Typically, we view it as an example of cruel optimism[40] whose utopian longing is naive and whose promise is undercut by the demand that we must inevitably fail in our efforts to transform aspiration into reality. Yet redemption is an important element of the habitual contraction that accompanies stories about child molestation, even if it is itself available only in a highly circumscribed way. That is, we want and need to see redemption. *And* we want that redemption to be failed or partial or haunted. So, for example, in the original *Times* story, we learn that the men involved in Justin Berry's exploitation and abuse are being brought to justice (indeed, he appears to help catch one of them). On the *Law and Order: SVU* episode "Web," clearly inspired by Berry's story, we know that the young pornographer who stands in for Justin will probably be rescued from the fan who kidnapped him, even as we are confirmed in our certainty that he's going to be damaged by his confession that he's "not okay." Then there's Oprah's "Bravo, bravo." We know (and we want to know this, too; we want the surety of this knowledge) the odds are that even the kids who've been saved will have problems, even if we celebrate their courage in coming forward. According to dominant beliefs, those who, like Justin Berry, were directly abused will likely end up with developmental problems, especially related to intimacy and sex. But even the kids who are saved a priori by the efforts of law enforcement, task forces, researchers, Oprah, the SVU, Perverted Justice, *To Catch a Predator,* or just plain good parenting are made aware of the danger only just averted and which continues to threaten them. Passing through the crucible of technosexual abuse transforms children, but not for the better. It leaves its mark, and they join most of the rest of us to become, at least, paranoid, and, possibly, likely abusers (of drugs, themselves, or, of course, kids).

The Child operates in these stories about sex generally but online sex specifically to preclude redemption in specific iterations of the tale of innocence lost (that is, there are no stories about intergenerational sex where the kid ends up ok) and, importantly, by any virtual means (kids will never be better off having learned about sex online). This limited form of redemption is the cost we pay for our voyeurism. In Berry's story, his redemption operates, on the one hand, as part of the excuse and apology we provide ourselves for witnessing and participating in his exploitation. His effort to redeem himself, along with Eichenwald's adult aid, of course, is an essential element in the furtive but necessary looking (to see the horror, the good kid, the poor kid) we do at the semi-dirty pictures in the *New York Times* story or on Wikipedia (images that tease us with the promise that more are out there), or in the alarmed titillation or gossip we whisper about him (pornographer, entrepreneur, victim, queer). Part of the larger scripted drama of voyeurism and exploitation that everyone participates in when we engage these stories is overdetermined, in turn constraining and even erasing the chance that there might be other ways to be saved. As the virtualized Child, Berry's incomplete redemption congeals the potential for enlarging intimacy's scope—to intergenerational sex most definitely, but also to taking seriously the actual as opposed to imagined sexual lives of children and adolescents. For the purposes of my larger arguments about virtual intimacy, his story means we can't look to the virtual for other kinds of redemption—it can't redeem the limits of our imagination about identity, sex, and technology, and it can't enlarge our capacity for connection. The idea that we might turn to the virtual to redeem something about ourselves, to make different kinds of connection or belonging possible, is rendered unintelligible.

INNOCENCE LOST (AGAIN)

If Berry made out pretty well, with speaking gigs and consulting jobs, along with his ongoing tech entrepreneurship (all of which is necessarily haunted by the unspoken knowledge that he's damaged goods), the journalist who enabled this temporary salvation, Kurt Eichenwald, fared more poorly. Eichenwald was haunted by other things: by the knowledge of the kiddie porn industry; by Debbie Nathan's relentless criticisms; and by the apparent impossibility of maintaining journalistic standards while trying to save kids from predators, themselves, and us; and a secret. Not long after the *Times* editors amended Eichenwald's original story while giving him and themselves a pass on some of the larger issues at stake, the journalist left the paper to work for a new Condé Nast magazine, *Portfolio*. Yet his tenure there was short-lived, likely due in part to the still more complex portrait that emerged from the trial of Ken Gourlay, one of the men arrested in the wake of Berry's story. Apparently, in addition to the two thousand dollars he had initially paid (in an auction, remember) to meet Berry, there were other undisclosed monies, some that purchased pictures of Berry, others that paid for Web design services Berry rendered. Also troubling was evidence that some of this money had been used by Berry *after* Eichenwald had contacted him to revive his largely moribund JustinsFriends site, paying new underage models to appear. Indeed, membership to the site grew suddenly after Berry and Eichenwald's meeting, and Eichenwald would know because at this point he had administrative privileges to justinsfriends.com. On the surface, it would appear that Eichenwald, however unwittingly, aided Justin Berry, then in the age of majority, in the production of child pornography. Framed in this context, Berry's immunity deal takes on a different light, as does Eichenwald's retaining of a criminal defense lawyer (the same one representing Berry). When Eichenwald testified, he said he didn't remember.

He left *Portfolio* and no reason was given.

If this sounds like a rather sudden fall from grace for someone who had won the prestigious Payne Prize for this work, there's yet another wrinkle. Apparently, his claim to not remember wasn't simply the effort of a man trying to avoid possible criminal prosecution. It was instead, as NPR's *All Things Considered* scooped, the truth, resulting from a well-guarded secret. Though Eichenwald had publicly acknowledged being an epileptic, his epilepsy had begun to cause major neurological disruptions, including disruptions in his memory. He literally couldn't remember how much money he'd sent Berry or when he'd given it, though, apparently with his wife's accounting help, he revealed it was likely more than had been thus far speculated. The NPR story paints Eichenwald as a well-meaning man and passionate journalist who was caught up by forces more powerful than he, a maelstrom made more perilous because of a major disability (especially for a journalist!). And while Berry made it to shore, Eichenwald was still adrift, no longer working in the career he loved and was so good at, simply working on a book, needing his car's GPS to help him remember how to get home after picking up his kids from school.

Does he regret it? He pauses. While he laments his current situation, he was glad to have saved Justin and other kids. After all, they're our collective future.

FUCKING THE FUTURE

It's hard not to feel ambivalent in the wake of this story. Ruined lives, righteous posturing, ineffective laws, moral panics, and foreclosed possibilities. And, largely intact, is the figure of the Child and the narratives of futurity in which he figures and in whose service most of the fretting and desiring and future securing has been done. If this Child and the future that belongs to him overdetermines or, really, forecloses the potential for virtual intimacies to be more than failure or trouble, then I find myself altogether more sympathetic to Edelman's critique. Fuck the Child, indeed. Fuck the future, too. Justin Berry already has the hang of it. To fuck the future is to utilize technoscientific means toward erotic ends. It is, following Edelman, to reject reproductive futurism (and, less desirably for me, politics more generally). And it brings together cynicism and optimism, opportunism and entrepreneurial pluck.

Yet I'm not entirely resolved to this nihilism. I'd rather have my cruel optimism than none at all. Or, rather, I resolve to maintain a "queer optimism" that challenges the tenets of optimism itself. To support such an effort, though, requires turning to a different set of artifacts, ones that articulate another iteration of sex and technology, even as they still centrally feature the much-maligned webcam. Thus, I turn, in the next chapter, to the burgeoning world of Do It Yourself pornography and a few of the legal and perhaps less troubled, if only barely, porn stars of XTube.

CHAPTER FIVE

The *Élan Vital* of DIY Porn

IT'S ALIVE

I jump between sites.

I watch the cropped torso of a racially ambiguous young man with thick, muscular legs standing in front of a nondescript bathtub. He whispers, just audibly, "I'm so horny right now," rubbing his cock beneath red Diesel boxer briefs. He turns and pulls his underwear down, arching his back to reveal a hairy butt. He turns toward the camera again. He's modestly equipped, but his dick is very hard, and after only a few strokes, thick cum oozes from the tip of his penis. He pauses, trembles. And then he jerks off quickly; semen arcs towards the camera.

I switch to another tab on my browser and scan the screenshots of the men broadcasting on Cam4, a live pornographic webcam broadcasting site. I click on "Mister Chris," assuming that if nine hundred and fifteen other people are watching him, there must be something worth seeing. When the image resolves, two muscular young white men, one with a dark mop of hair and the other in a blue baseball cap are performing for a bossy audience: "chris kiss your hub," "start the action!" When the camera goes offline, I switch to "Tom_21cm." He's been online for more than an hour, and he says he's straight and waiting for the right girl to contact him on Skype. I try another, "26blkmuscle." He's also been online a while and doesn't seem to be in a hurry to cum, or maybe he's waiting on "tips," donations by the voyeurs watching him.

Impatient, I open another tab. I watch a Creative Commons licensed submission in the 2007 Do-It-Yourself porn festival, CUM-2CUT. Created according to a lottery-assigned rubric—"Christian Porn"—the video features a pierced male punk in wedding drag who enters a church, ecstatically announces his desire for Jesus to a tattooed minister, who then pisses on the sub supplicant. The minister sends the young apostle to eat the body of Christ, a bearded dyke suspended on a cross, who appears to suffer very little during an eager session of cunnilingus.

What do these scenes have in common? Each represents a small part of a vast gay pornographic archive that depends on the active engagement of everyday people. Each represents a Do-It-Yourself (DIY) approach to pornographic self-representation, and marks the degree to which pornography has become increasingly defined by Web 2.0 tenets: user-generated content is produced and flows among and through diverse networks of users who collectively shape meaning and value.

These expanding ecologies of DIY porn are simultaneously explosive and ordinary. That is, DIY porn shows how porn has become an "open" practice not limited to commercial or corporate interests. The widespread and relatively inexpensive availability of a range of image capture technologies (from digital cameras to webcams and cell phones) has democratized the ability to produce and exchange a wide array of sexual representations, while also challenging the images and commercialism of "industrial porn," the multibillion dollar interests that shape our shared pornographic imaginations, that arouses for profit. This is not to say that DIY porn necessarily upends the established pornographic order. In fact, much of it, as in the first two examples above, is altogether more banal. Putting aside the preponderance of grainy or boring videos, even those videos that achieve the pornographic effects their authors intended, that is, arousal, do not necessarily break new political or aesthetic ground. Put crudely, very few of the many, many DIY-documented cumshots or a viewer's accompanying masturbatory success necessarily approaches the explosive promise of Lacanian *jouissance*. Nonetheless, this chapter contends that gay DIY porn offers important ways for thinking about the liveliness of sexual representations and exchanges.

Each of the above scenes therefore evinces what I call in this chapter "the *élan vital* of DIY porn." In what follows, I appropriate philosopher Henri Bergson's *élan vital* to express the creative and generative capacities and effects of gay DIY porn. I thereby suggest that rather than function as evidence of "pornified"[1] cultural values that reflect the deadening of our existing or future interpersonal, broadly social, and selfsame intimacies, gay DIY porn represents a generative aliveness, an active contribution to and elaboration of networked bodies and desires. I'm arguing in short, and not a little playfully, that DIY porn is possessed of a vital force.

ÉLAN VITAL

It's unlikely Henri Bergson imagined that his *élan vital* would be metaphorically invoked to discuss the evolution and aliveness of gay male pornographic images. He used the idea in his 1907 book *Creative Evolution* to comment on the biological sciences of his time, criticizing their reductionist views of life and matter and suggesting that they had not grasped the animating principles of life. Although he is often grouped, disparagingly, with "vitalist" thinkers and philosophies, Bergson's views were, in fact, distinct. For example, he did not believe, as other vitalists did, in an animating immaterial force, or a transcendent divine will, that operated in addition to material ones. As Michael Vaughan observes, for Bergson *élan vital*

> signifies a force different in kind to matter conceived mechanistically or deterministically, and this "force" is nothing more than that very same matter conceived intuitively: as active, as creative, as itself vital—the very qualities that a mechanistic materialism effaces when it isolates superposable parts and treats as quantifiable and repeatable what is really continuous qualitative change. Élan vital as the organization of matter neither implies nor requires the action of an immaterial agent; it requires the conception of matter *as* agency.[2]

I sidestep the question of whether Bergson was a vitalist (but see Vaughan) or whether vitalism makes for good science (it doesn't, although it poses ethically important questions about how to think aliveness and materiality). Rather, I am inspired by his conception of *élan vital* to think through the liveliness of gay DIY pornography, to the creative initiative as well as the constraining pressures that shape its production and circulation. As in so much of this book, I am interested in generativity; *élan vital* therefore serves as another way of framing the "movement of differentiation,"[3] the capacity to move and be moved, and the ways change operates to enliven life.

Élan vital thus helps to frame gay DIY pornography as a vital force affecting and affected by transformations in, most obviously, sexual mores, as well as the politics of representation and the growth of network cultures. It refers to an aliveness both extant and immanent, to gathered energies that press on collective and individual beliefs and desires, and to other energies not yet distributed or in circulation. It refers as well to an innate capacity for a kind of pornographic self-sovereignty (or in the touchy-feely language of twelve step programs and the New Age movement, "self-actualization"), for the creative transformation of one's life into porn and/or art without, hopefully, carrying too much of the hierarchical and dualistic baggage that attends either of those categories, that blurs or makes sticky the lines between high and low, elevated and carnal.[4] Of course, these practices of creative self-making and the profligate circulation of these performative embodiments that come with the possibilities of Web 2.0, don't operate outside boundaries or constraints. I discuss these limits, ontological, political, aesthetic, and otherwise, below. But they do emphasize the capacity to choose, act, and create, signaling affective, political, and ontological orientations that commit to freedom as practice and process, as immanently available, even when it comes to porn.

DIY PORN/GAY PORN HISTORIES

Curator, artist, and scholar Katrien Jacobs, in her comprehensive book *Netporn: DIY Web Culture and Sexual Politics,*[5] examines the aesthetic and political dimensions of DIY porn. Porn reflects transformations in digital media technologies and in how we understand and employ the sexually expressed and expressive body. For her, new DIY netporn practices open spaces for the progressive and activist construction of alternative or queer sexual subjectivities and images, and they draw the attention of state interests who survey and censor these new Web publics. In Jacobs's view, DIY porn therefore epitomizes the participatory qualities of what Henry Jenkins has dubbed "convergence culture," in which the lines between producer, consumer, and fan blur. For Jacobs the widespread participation in online sex publics and the proliferation of "micro-porn spaces," the wide range of sexual and

identitarian niches available online, evokes Paulo Virno's theories of
the "multitude":

> Multitudes create mobility and escape from corporate indus-
> tries and the exploitation of workers, where they would be
> seen as dead labor within the exchange economy. Multi-
> tudes do not adhere to older definitions of work masses
> nor critical masses that can overthrow the system. Multi-
> tudes are characterized by the transformation of produc-
> tion through the application of technical knowledge and
> socialized intelligence.[6]

Online DIY porn cultures are "lubricants" for social actors to
engage new media and one another.[7] Jacobs situates these engagements
in a broader politics of sexuality; as she puts it, "[These] generations
of porn users have helped define sexual tolerance, sex debates, and
revolutions in the face of social backlash."[8]

Gay and queer men's specific participation in and contributions
to networked porn are likewise situated within broader social histories, pornographic and otherwise. Given the ways in which gay
men formed intimate networks in the context of state monitoring
and repression, as well as the social backlash Jacobs describes above,
one might argue that gay men helped to innovate today's ubiquitous
social networking.[9] These histories illustrate changing definitions and
anxieties about pornography and emergent publics alike. Certainly, by
the advent of technologies of mass reproduction, namely, photography
and film, recognizable and self-conscious subcultures of same-sex desiring men already existed in most major urban areas. These prototypi-
cally gay men were, like others in the late nineteenth century, already
consumers of sexually explicit images. And some became producers
as well, although as Thomas Waugh observes, many important figures
in the early production of now-canonical gay iconography were artists who, such as Baron Wilhelm von Gloeden, produced, more or
less surreptitiously, erotic images under the banner of art.[10] These art
images entered into pornographic circulation via particular routes, post
cards and mail order catalogs. Many of these artists were self-trained
(von Gloeden began as a hobbyist photographer, for example), early
antecedents to a DIY trend that has continued throughout much of
the history of gay representation.[11] Of course, hardcore images of

sexual acts between men were necessarily DIY because there were no conditions for its legal production until the relaxing of obscenity laws in the early 1960s. Most hardcore pornography was produced and circulated through the gift economies of personal networks or gray and black markets. And notably, throughout these pornographic histories, there have been some remarkably stable preoccupations with images of youth and hegemonic masculinity. When actual sex acts were depicted, these practices were, for much of gay porn's history, also quite stable: masturbation, oral, and anal sex.

There have been a number of significant developments since: most porn's effective legalization (the 1960s), a brief period in which it entered the mainstream (porn chic in the '70s with films such as the straight *Deep Throat* and the gay *Boys in the Sand*), the shift to video,[12] AIDS, transnational porn labor pools (in the former Soviet Union and the Global South), the proliferation of niche genres (twinks, bears, daddies, fratboys, fisting, bareback, etc.), the digital revolution (there have been two—one in the late '90s and the other in the early aughts—which saw the proliferation of a range of sites by amateurs and professionals alike, and the second from the birth of Web 2.0 to now). Gay porn has been essential to the interpellation of gay identities at least since the 1970s. In ten years of research, every same-sex desiring man I've spoken with who has come of age since the advent of the Internet has identified encounters with online porn as an important, even formative, element in the development of his sexual identity.

But by the mid-1980s most of the pornography produced for and distributed to gay men moved away from the independently produced and often cinematically compelling work epitomized by Wakefield Poole, Jean Daniel Cadinot, and others toward a corporate or industrial porn model.[13] While industrial porn is distinguished by a range of factors—methods of financing, production staff, professional models, distribution networks, etc.—at base it is shaped by an economic bottom line: industrial porn arouses for profit. It represents the corporate production and management of desire, and predictably employs a capitalistic approach to the use-value of the bodies it displays, that is, the labor is cheap, flexible, and disposable.

Anti-porn feminists point to these elements as evidence of structural injustice built into modern pornographic enterprises.[14] And in addition to reproducing sexual and gender inequality, anti-porn perspectives point to the deleterious effects pornography has on our intimate lives—why grapple with the difficulties of our relationships with

others when porn provides all of the pleasure with none of the nego-
tiation and compromise (porn never has a headache). In the same vein,
other critics and researchers decry the harmful effects pornographic
images have on the sexual identity development of youth, pointing
out the ways such images celebrate hierarchical difference and promote
unrealistic, and unhealthy, images of the body.[15] Still others suggest that
porn has taken the place of more tangible and messy intimacies with
our sexual partners.[16] These, then, are the dead or deadening effects
of pornography.

But the widespread consumption of porn, the creation of new
genres, the leaking of porn into popular culture, all make anti-porn
arguments more problematic. How do anti-porn feminists account for
amateur self-pornographers turned entrepreneurs of the first Web porn
boom, many of them tech-savvy women? How do they account for the
proliferation of digital DIY porn in particular? Is *every* pornographic
image produced by a sexually traumatized victim of capitalist exploitation and false consciousness? The everyday production of pornographic
images across a vast range of social contexts instead suggests porn is
an altogether more open and vital rather than closed and dead force.

OPEN PORN

The widespread availability and ease of use of a wide range of digital
media technologies have made porn more democratically accessible,
or open. The vast array of user-generated content—Web groups, cam
sex, peer-to-peer (p2p) exchange and piracy, blogs, activist or fan sites,
or the crowd-sourced content of XTube and its clones[17]—have particularly empowered marginal sexual identities and embodiments to
enter into pornographic production and exchange. Jacobs and Feona
Attwood,[18] for example, each point to a range of altsex sites, from the
nerdy, goth, and punk chicks of SuicideGirls and Nerve, to the emergence of gay bear subcultures in a range of global contexts as evidence
of netporn's "exuberant" democratic possibilities. Peter Lehman points
to a user-generated precursor of Xtube, Voyeurweb, which began in
1997, and looks specifically to the ways the site illustrates the changing representation of the penis which have historically fallen into only
a handful of categories: "the desirable big dick in porn, the pathetic
small penis the butt of the joke in humor, the medically normative
penis measured in inches, and the tasteful aesthetic penis of high art."[19]
While many images of penises "replicate rather than challenge" these

tropes and discourses,[20] other users' images and "comments challenge and expand those norms, calling them into question and exposing them for what they are: culturally, historically, and ideologically constructed categories open to change."[21] The site therefore makes space for the underrepresented dick, the shy, curved, or humble member. Tatiana Bazzichelli, co-organizer of the CUM2CUT independent porn festival I discuss in more detail below, meanwhile imagines an explicitly activist porn of the future that is pro-sex, explicitly queer, and collaborative, and that operates to contribute to a social-sexual commons.

Opening porn to a range of social actors and representational techniques, digital DIY porn cultures render more sexual realities and possibilities "on/scene."[22] This openness is moreover shaped by the way much DIY porn makes commercialism stutter. Online gay DIY porn is alive in part through the ways it resists the deadening organizing profit motive of industrial porn; rather than arouse for profit, much DIY porn circulates in gift economies.

ALT SEX/ALT ECONOMY

Although a number of early Web entrepreneurs leveraged sexual representations into profitable (and increasingly commercial paysites), Web groups (Usenet and later groups found at Yahoo or Google), p2p exchanges, image posting sites such as Voyeurweb, and Web 2.0 sites like XTube demonstrate the ways DIY porn frequently circulates within alternative economies of exchange. These are gift economies in which people offer themselves as freely given pornographic gifts, and thereby create cycles of interaction and reciprocation. A classically anthropological interest, gift economies are distinct from market economies in a number of ways. Here, I emphasize only one: in a market economy relationships between consumer and producer conclude with a transaction. Gift economies, by contrast, produce ongoing cycles of exchange and reciprocation that effect and reinforce bonds between groups. In the case of DIY porn, in exchange for their pornographic gifts, posters receive a range of feedback, from suggestions for future videos, to gratitude, to other more material gifts including goods such as clothes or cameras, even money. They also receive pornographic gifts of their own, as they inspire others to participate in this gift economy.

Moreover, by sidestepping the economic overhead of commercial porn—DIY amateurs don't have to pay themselves, other models, fluffers, and so on—part of the pleasure-value of these sites arises from their participatory flavor. Those who post videos for example often do so out of a desire to share, to receive the input and feedback of other users. And while some posters are obviously exhibitionists who derive pleasure from others' voyeurism, others self-consciously intervene in established pornographic orders by posting creative or unusual videos (more on these below). The value of pornographic artifacts in Web 2.0 sites like XTube is thereby determined by factors not wholly tied to monetization. Some of these factors are relatively obvious and reflect the quality and originality of the video (Was the video clearly filmed? Does it afford a pleasurable or interesting view of a body?). The volume of videos a user posts shapes value, too; a relatively high volume of posting creates a fan base that offers steady interaction and feedback. Value is also shaped by whether a user develops (represents) a particularly evocative sexual identity (this is often, though not always, determined by whether or not posters reveal their faces) or make exciting contributions to a particular genre (hunks, piss, solo, etc.). From aesthetic and political points of view, value is thus produced by one's ability to work with limited materials, to creatively rework and expand the pornographic imagination, and to seduce a public through gifts more or less freely given.[23]

SHARING SEX

Bryanterry is the pseudonymous screen name of a twenty-two-year-old college student. Over the last four years, he's uploaded, as of this writing, 235 videos to his XTube account. He has more than twelve thousand "friends" and ten thousand subscribers. His videos have been viewed ten million times. His uploads follow a relatively consistent format. They all feature him alone in a bathroom or dorm room masturbating until he ejaculates. Although his early videos featured his face, albeit partially obscured with blindfolds or masks, most of his videos do not; he does offer unobstructed views of the rest of his body. The early videos show a penchant for light bondage, but the preponderance of subsequent uploads fetishize "gear": clothing articles, usually related to sports such as jockstraps, swimsuits, and wrestling singlets. Increasingly, he posts videos in which he masturbates in or with gifts—silk shirts, boxers, moccasins, jockstraps, and more—his fans have already provided or that they plan to purchase after he appears in them. Occasionally, he uses a dildo to engage in ass play or uses a sex toy such as a Fleshjack, a popular masturbation sleeve. Viewers frequently hear his whispered voice expressing excitement and pleasure: "Oh fuck, I'm so horny," "That feels so good," "Do you like it?" are common refrains. Although the videos adhere to a general formula—masturbating until ejaculation, often in or with fetishized clothes, the videos nonetheless consistently evoke praise, and he continues to upload them; they are vital.

Bryanterry says he began posting videos after a friend suggested XTube as a place where he could post sexually suggestive images that social networking sites like Myspace did not permit. The videos

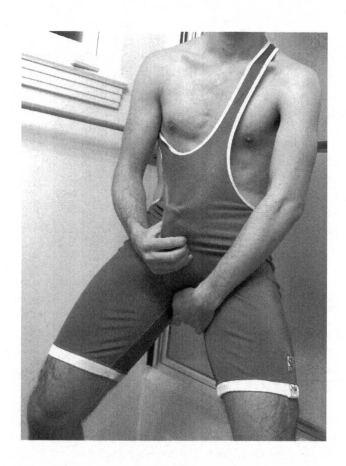

FIGURE 5.1. Bryanterry

became a means for him to explore and express aspects of his sexual identity he felt awkward about sharing with others. In his own words, "I love having a way to do things I might be embarrassed to do with other people, or play out fantasies that I'm curious about that might seem weird or different to actual potential boyfriends." He also began to take an exhibitionist pleasure in the effects he had on others. His own participation in the sexual gift economy of gay DIY porn sites like XTube was itself inspired by others' contributions and his own sexual imagination: "They are inspired from others and myself." When I asked him if he had some examples, he couldn't think of specific ones. Rather, he emphasized the videos' realness—"I loved how real they were"—and an exciting collectivity—"I liked how there were people like me making really hot videos and getting to turn people on from all over the world . . . [I]t's basically a culmination of videos I saw." The impetus for creating new videos also comes in turn from the encouragement and interaction his videos generate among his fans.

Although he recognizes the possibility of leveraging the popularity of his videos for a "pro-amateur" career in which he could generate revenue from his videos or branch out into quasi-commercial markets, Bryanterry chooses to continue to offer his videos for free. He says he does this for two reasons. First, going pro-am would, in his view, require him to reveal his identity, and he worries about hurting his friends and family. And second, he believes that by giving his videos away for free, more people are able to enjoy them and that his openness increases his audience's, and his own, pleasure. He says, "I feel it's kinda hotter anyway to give them away for free and see how people react. They might pay anyway, but still I think more people enjoy my videos because it's a great way for them to get off and it's free and open." For Bryanterry the fact that his videos are self-produced—he uses a point and shoot camera and his webcam—means that he is in control of his own sexual representation and can interact directly with his fans. This, he feels, contributes to a sense of authenticity distinct from the "fake" or "cheesy" offerings of mainstream commercial gay pornography.

Bryanterry clearly distinguishes his own videos from the material produced by commercial porn. By remaining anonymous he is afforded relative freedom to explore and express a range of his sexual desires and practices, as well as respond to requests from his fans. In this context his sexual performances have become an important part of his individual sexual self-definition,[24] although he indicates that he might remove his videos if this anonymity were threatened. Unlike commercial porn, Bryanterry's videos are organized by a noncommercial impetus; he arouses for his own and others' pleasure. This is not to say that his contributions operate outside all economic concerns. He does, for example, receive gifts, largely in the form of clothing and gear, and also some unsolicited money. He understands these gifts as perks and not as animating ends; he doesn't make videos to make money. Still, these donations do appear to impel him to create more videos: "There haven't been that many significant donations, but sometimes people are generous when they buy gear from me like underwear. I have a thing for underwear and gear, as you can probably tell, so I actually like donations and selling gear to get more to show off in videos. It turns me on!"

Importantly, unlike other XTube users or user-generated social networking sites more generally, he doesn't use the sexual persona he has created on XTube as a way to make face-to-face connections. Indeed, he says that he does not meet people from the site, a paradoxically conservative position, given his commitment to documenting fantasies. Although his videos have affective and embodied results, if the comments posted on his profile page are any indication, these intimacies remain for him strictly on screen: "I don't meet up with people from the site, no matter how tempted I am sometimes, because the world is a dangerous place and I'd rather take my chances meeting people through other channels." Thus, although Bryanterry's videos are "real" expressions of his sexual desires, he also understands them as "fantasy and fun." In this way his videos blur the lines between categories of authentica,[25] the widespread taste for mediated images of the ordinary life and the naked bodies that might inhabit them, and realcore, the superficially unmediated depiction of "real people with real desires, having real sex in real places."[26]

MYSTERY PORN

If Bryanterry's videos evoke something of the liveliness of gay DIY Web cultures in the ways they depend on feelings of inspiration and participate in economies of gift exchange, then the videos by The Black Spark suggest how gay DIY porn can interrupt the narrative and aesthetic limits of commercial gay porn. Although historical analyses of gay porn reveal the ways the genre has often blurred the lines between art and pornography,[27] contemporary commercial porn only rarely evinces reflexive or "aesthetic" impulses.[28] And insofar as so much gay pornography since the 1990s has been produced within the rubric of the genre "amateur," the narrative elements, however flimsy, that structured gay pornography as "features" have almost entirely disappeared.[29] Instead, the majority of gay pornographic content follows a predictable script of sexual coupling captured by equally formulaic techniques of visual representation. The choreography of sexual action typically goes something like this: brief dialogue (though this is easily and frequently omitted), kissing (ditto), oral sex, preliminary anal penetration through fingering or rimming, anal sex, and ejaculation.[30] The filming, framing, and editing that capture these sexual encounters are likewise limited.[31] In a typical depiction of anal sex, for example, the camera captures the initial moment of penetration and then focuses (often through the use of multiple cameras) on angles that would normally be hidden from view during actual intercourse. Cameras are positioned underneath the actors, for instance, or laterally posterior, and the performers themselves assume unnatural, or at least very awkward, positions to maximize the visual pleasure of the viewer (in interviews some porn stars describe how they "cheat the camera" by, for example, arching one's back). Most commercial gay pornography emphasizes the friction of intercourse and makes the money shot its inevitable outcome.[32] And while fucking and/or ejaculation are likewise the teleology of much DIY porn, the particular ways in which these are expressed vary widely and offer important counterpoints to the representational and narrative ideologies of commercial pornography.

The videos of The Black Spark illustrate how these conventions can be resisted. The videos juxtapose disjointed, highly aestheticized sexual scenes set to a range of evocative contemporary music, from American indiepop band Chester French to the British New Wave revivalists La Roux. The videos are semi-serialized (they are sometimes referred to as "chapters"), building on one another while also recycling images and scenes. Superimposed or scrolling text plays an important role. Text encourages the interaction of the videos' audience, asking viewers to "email theblackspark@gmail.com" and "add me on Facebook," and sometimes the texts repeat the videos' titles, themselves often taken from the titles of the songs that provide their soundtracks. Most importantly, text narrativizes the videos.[33] Taken together, the images, music, and text evoke mysterious narratives of sexual loneliness, addiction, loss, betrayal, and obsession. At the same time, especially through the persistent use of masks, they suggest a fantasy world of superheroes for whom sex is a weapon or curse. From yet another, complementary, angle, they take an experimental or meta tack, in the manner of David Lynch or the television show *Lost,* to the tropes of conventional pornographic fare, at once celebrating and deconstructing hegemonic masculinity and "dude sex."[34]

The first video, titled "Not Over You," opens with a closely cropped image of one of the performers, face concealed by a white *commedia del arte* mask, showering, a glowstick in his mouth. Juxtaposed over his image is the text: "Who is The Black Spark." A quick edit cuts to a closely framed shot of the hand of a figure inserting an orange glowstick into his rectum.

The tightly cropped frame, with saturated, heavily contrasted orange and olive hues, then cuts again, first to more text—"I live alone"—and then to black and white images of a living space crowded with musical equipment. Another edit follows, this time to what appears to be the same masked figure masturbating in a bathtub; here the orange glowstick in the water casts an eerie light on the long white nose of the Pulcinella mask. This image is the first to indi-

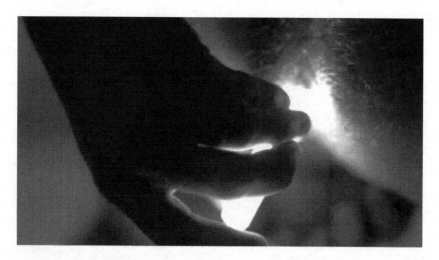

FIGURE 5.2. The Black Spark's aestheticism.

cate that these videos are not produced by the figure in the frame because the camera pans from left to right. And again, text appears superimposed, "Lust is the source/Of my power." All the while, the song "Not Over You," by the band Chester French plays. The lyrics underscore a narrative of loss: "Late night, long flight, sleep till we land/Hotel, dead cell, sun bathes the sand/Met you at school, made me your fool/Always just out of reach/Flying away, trying to make this my day/I'm hung up again on a peach/I try to say what I gotta say/But I'm not through/I try to do what I gotta do/But I'm not over you." The plaintive "I'm not over you" accompanies further cuts and juxtapositions of image and text, first to a scene that includes a second figure (now suggesting at least three collaborators), followed by the overlaid words "deceived by my own illusion and pride." Here, cool greens and blues, along with the bright halo created by a string of LED lights in the center of the frame, illuminate a scene of anal sex. Our masked protagonist is being fucked; he lies passively on the bed, turning his head to face the camera. Following a brief pan comes another scene of anal sex, which although it takes place on the same bed (viewers see the same brick wall in the background), the glowsticks and LEDS that created such rich colors are now absent. And for the first time, more than a minute into the video, we see the face of a

FIGURE 5.3. The Black Spark as Pulcinella?

man being fucked; we hear his voice: "fuck me, oh fuck me." Another text reads "He still hurt me." Although the similar background and the continuity of sexual acts suggest this is our protagonist unmasked, we do not know for sure.

The video continues for more than two minutes in much the same way, including other dramatic images often unrelated to sex, like a glass filled with burning paper or of a scorpion, stinger alert and poised to strike. When the music cuts out during the last seconds of the video, only the slapping sound of sex remains and a voice grunts, "Oh yeah, fuck, Oh yeah."

Subsequent entries in the series likewise surreally mix aestheticized eroticism, hardcore sex, evocative musical soundtracks, and often-idiosyncratic text (words are misspelled, strangely capitalized, or mashed up) with sometimes random images (such as a polarized image of brushing teeth or the aforementioned scorpion). One soft-focus scene even suggests a kidnapping by a ninja. Masked figures fuck in parks and hallways, and once in a video store with gay porn films visible on the shelves. Indoor sex scenes are often lit solely with flickering LEDs. Sexually, there's an emphasis on oral cum-shots, cum-eating, and masturbation, although there are also a number of scenes of bareback sex. Nearly everyone wears a mask of one sort or another—the white *commedia del arte* mask plays an important role, as does what I describe as terrorist-dude drag, in which a baseball cap and bandana obscure the figure's face. A superhero motif is supported through, in an early video, a quick cut image of Spiderman, as well as through the buff bodies of performers, and the repeated use of the word *power* in the superimposed text, as in, especially, "Chapter 1.5" (the third video in the series): "Elsewhere a villain is born/he will take your power/up his ass/down his throat/ now he has stolen mine/i LOST focus/the great power was swallowed" (*sic*). With as many as three men in some scenes, it also becomes increasingly clear that The Black Spark's videos are a collective effort.

In an interview with Thesword.com, a blog associated with the pay-per-view gay porn site, The Naked Sword, The Black Spark, who has maintained his anonymity, elaborates the vision that animates his hybrid DIY porn contributions. He also reveals a bit about their production, noting that there are a number of different men, or "sparks," of which he is only one. He and one other (unfilmed) man shoot the videos. In the interview, he presents the videos as a means to explore his sexual desires, as a counterpoint to the banality of commercial porn, and as a political challenge to cultural expectations about sex and sexual propriety.

However, it appears that his real aspiration is to make art.

Like Bryanterry, The Black Spark expresses a belief that this virtual medium enabled him to explore his real desires, desires that others wanted to "fence in." The videos therefore function as a kind of sexual therapy. He contrasts the aestheticism of his own work with the images in mainstream porn, which he complains is "boring." He nostalgically refers to a classic gay pornographic feature, *The Other Side of Aspen,* saying, "I'd get off to something [like that] before I would any of the new stuff. I mean, the guys are hot, but it's all the same. Personally, I need more." Like many of his fans, who wonder whether his work should really be categorized as erotic art rather than porn, The Black Spark himself expresses ambivalence on this point—"I worry about it being considered porn everyday." His desire to blur boundaries goes farther. Unlike Bryanterry, for example, he also understands his intervention as political. He wants "to break some barriers." When the interviewer asks, "Is that your main intention with Black Spark then, to break barriers? To challenge censorship?" The Black Spark responds, "I started doing this for a lot of reasons, but sure, challenging people's preconceived notions is a big part of it." Later, he continues, "If I can make people talk about censorship and acceptance, then I'm doing my job."

But in this heady aspirational mix, The Black Spark's challenge to pornographic conventions and cultural expectations are really a means to even higher ends. Specifically, they are a way to garner attention and funding to support two features, one an independent film he hopes to circulate at film festivals and the other a sexually explicit origin story for his hypersexualized masked alter ego.

And the videos, for all their apparently self-conscious interventions, present an altogether more ambivalent portrait. One obvious contradiction arises in his interview. He wants to maintain his privacy while also being a sexual exhibitionist. Expressing a desire to challenge assumptions about sexual propriety doesn't yet mean he's committed to risking his own. And while the videos' surreal "artiness" is certainly unusual within the context of either more mainstream or DIY fare, they don't upend pornographic conventions. The videos, after all, feature a number of well-endowed, physically toned, young white men, whose bodies are so similar as to be almost interchangeable, especially when their faces are absent, masked, or otherwise obscured. They also emphasize sexual acts like facial cum shots, cum-eating, and bareback sex, which, if video downloads and sales are any indication, are among the most valued sexual images of the pornographic moment. In economic terms, these videos may not arouse for profit in a manner identical to the representational logics of commercial porn, but they do employ sexual representations for economic aims, even if those aims are directed toward the production of art. And how sophisticated are the videos' formal interventions? On the one hand, I found myself entranced by the use of light and color in the videos—light becomes sensuously material, it penetrates bodies, refracting the ways watching porn screens is a form of touch in which the affective power of the image works directly on the body. On the other hand, I wondered how many of these effects were intended and how many were accidental. I found myself identifying with one of my informants, himself a recent contributor to online DIY pornographic culture, who put it simply, "Would I watch these videos if there wasn't any sex in them? The answer is no." Without the sexual content, The Black Spark's videos fall within the scope of another genre of DIY participatory culture, fan video music remixes.

Whether or not The Black Spark's videos actually represent a serious artistic or political alternative, it's clear from his interview and from the many hundreds of comments by fans that the videos participate in the formation of a pornographic "taste culture" that identifies itself as a sophisticated counterpoint to mainstream or other DIY porn and in which "aesthetics is evoked as a form of ethics."[35]

The indieporn festival CUM2CUT, to which I now turn, offers a more coherent political philosophy of DIY sexual representations and likewise works toward simultaneously elaborating both pornographic aesthetics and ethics.

HACKING PORN

In the CUM2CUT indieporn festival DIY porn is framed as a hacktivist practice that brings a punk political sensibility to sedimented narratives and images of sexual bodies and identities. Emphasizing the ties that bind queer and hacker cultures and sensibilities, especially the shared desires to simultaneously resist and open normative imperatives, the festival invites participants to produce short pornographic films over a four-day period. As the organizers write on their Web page, "In this context, queer means to express sexuality beyond the boundaries of identity and to cross the limits of fixed genders and stereotypes. At

the same time, the idea of being queer is closely connected with the
D.I.Y. attitude: CUM2CUT wants to encourage everyone to express
themselves using their bodies and media from an independent point
of view, thereby creating new experimental queer languages."[36] Participants were assigned a pornographic category through a lottery. In
the 2007 festival held in Berlin, which added a "Pr0n"[37] competition
to the program, lottery categories included gothic porn, horror porn,
and futuristic porn, among others. Participants also had to adhere to
a handful of rules: certain images had to appear in all the films (the
"@" symbol and a city map of Berlin), as did particular audio (the
sentence "I used to have such a good imagination" had to be said
and the sound of a slap made audible). Films were screened as part
of the Berlin Porn Festival and queer filmmakers and pornographers
selected winners.

In 2007 winning films included the first prize "Who ever could
imagine Christianity was so fulfilling?" and, sharing second prize, "Wild
bore hunting style II" and "Make my socialism creme filled." The
categories in which the films were produced were, respectively, Christian Porn, College Horror Porn, and Socialist Porn. Interestingly, of
the three, only the first features any explicit sexual content. Indeed,
by working to queerly hack pornography the festival winners contest
what counts as sexual arousal, ostensibly the organizing principle of
pornography. In the first film, which I described in brief at the opening
of this chapter, a young man in a white dress (evocative of Madonna
circa "Like a Virgin") walks down a Berlin street angrily speaking into
his phone and expressing his determination to go to church: "I'm
finding this church. I'm going there and you can't stop me. You can't
stop me." And a moment later, "Listen to me, you little bitch, but
now I just don't know anymore. And I'm joining the church, and you
know what, there's nothing in hell you can do about it!" He holds
his Berlin map, on which a note reads "Find Jesus @ Mariannenplatz."
Arriving at the St. Thomas Church, he exclaims in relief, "Hallelujah,
I'm going to church." Inside what is obviously not the real church,
a punk rock priest confronts him, "Are you ready to accept Jesus as
your Lord and Savior?" Replying in the affirmative, the priest invites
our white-dressed and black-bewigged protagonist to kneel before him.
What appear to be two (grown) altar boys stand behind the priest
and a small table with a framed image of the Virgin Mary. The priest
then baptizes the supplicant with pee, who ecstatically proclaims, "Oh
Jesus! I can feel Jesus within me!" The priest then exhorts, "Now

eat the body of Christ!" gesturing toward a bare breasted but mustachioed woman with arms bound to a makeshift crucifix. The cunnilingus that follows is accompanied by synthesized music that evokes a lo-fi pornographic soundtrack and is cut with images of the altar boys performing (likely simulated) oral sex on the punk priest and later (unsimulated) fellatio on a crucifix. In its representations of drag, same- and cross-gender contact, kinky sex, and religious imagery the video is a playful equal opportunity offender. It subverts pornographic expectations—no beefy bodies, fake tits, or money shots here—and hacks religious language and iconography as queer.

The second prizewinners hack porn more abstractly. In "Wild bore," the filmmakers open with an image of a plug being mated to a socket, an image they recycle several times during their video. Supporting the "college horror porn" theme, much of the film is so dark as to be almost unviewable and is accompanied by ominous, growling ambient noise. Scenes of cars speeding along dark Berlin streets are cut with a murky image of a figure whipping the body of a Trabbi, the famous and often-derided East German automobile, with a cat o' nine tails while offscreen voices giggle and whisper in German. The scene continues for a moment and the soundtrack is replaced with the increasingly audible sounds of women moaning with (we assume) sexual pleasure. More visual cuts follow as the now pornographic soundtrack continues to an androgynous figure thrusting a pipe in and out of a sidewalk and to more images of male plugs mated to female sockets. As the moans intensify, another cut follows a shopping cart as it accelerates down a dark street until it crashes into another cart thrust from an alley. The crash is followed by a brief cut to an explosion that could only have come from a bombastic Hollywood actioner (the credits don't reveal the source). Another abstract scene follows. A sign labeled "SUPER SEKSI KÄSEBROT" points to a plate and a barely discernible sandwich. The super sexy cheesy bread is impaled with sparklers, which are then lit. One of the performers proceeds to eat the fireworks sandwich. The screen fades to black for a few seconds until a sort of coda appears. "Wild bore hunting" concludes with an androgynous figure sitting on a toilet, peeing and then pulling on the nearby roll of toilet paper on which appears some of the material required by the competition: "I used to have such a good imagination" . . . @ . . . and a map of the formerly divided city. Alerted to an abrasive clacking, the figure looks down between his/her legs to find a mechanical toy caterpillar humping a mechanical duck.

In "Make my socialism creme filled," scenes from "Perversion for Profit," a well-known 1965 anti-porn film narrated by journalist George Putnam that decries pornography as a threat to American culture and civilization writ large and links obscenity to communist conspiracies, is sped up, slowed down, and intercut with scenes of a perverse baking party in which masked and dragged up revelers use dildos to whip cream that they spread on each other and a socialist cake cum effigy graced by Lenin's silhouetted head. As with the other festival videos, there's an abundance of loose and aggressive playfulness with none of the studied sensuality of The Black Spark's videos.

The CUM2CUT winners are choppy, rough, in short, punk, and hardly erotic at all. But the point of hacking porn isn't necessarily to create new forms of queer eroticism but perhaps to open up representations of sex and gender more broadly. Or, put differently, they evince the eroticism that is virtual to the everyday world, the immanent kink waiting everywhere: in church (perhaps obviously), or in maps, cars, shopping carts, whipped cream (again obviously), and dinner parties. Their interventions go beyond the obvious phallic symbolism of the pipe or socket in "Wild bore" to imagine sex/orgasm as crashing shopping carts or as an orgiastic scene of socialist play and consumption. The sexual body is not normatively enfleshed, then, rather it is made cyborg, rearranging and discovering new ways to make intimate contact or get off.

In a brief essay, "On Hacktivist Pornography and Networked Porn," CUM2CUT co-founder Tatiana Bazzichelli optimistically frames the work produced in the festival, and indie queer porn more generally, as a "porn of the future" that makes pornographic production a part of everyday life.[38] Describing her vision for a hacktivist porn practice, she evokes the playfully antagonistic interventions of Dada and Fluxus: "In 1972 Wolf Vostell, one of the pioneers of video art, happenings and the Fluxus movement, wrote in a postcard: 'Duchamp has qualified the object into art. I have qualified life into art.'"[39] In order to critically explore and challenge both the intimate and structural pressures that shape gender and sexuality, and to create sex-positive images and cultures, Bazzichielli suggests, "*We should qualify porn into life.*"[40] CUM-2CUT was therefore an effort to rework porn as an "open concept, as a new way of living the city space creating a network of people through pornography, and an occasion to disrupt the boundaries and the limits of sexuality."[41] Unlike other indie porn fests such as Boston's You Oughta Be in Pictures or Seattle's Humpday, CUM2CUT has an explicitly queer pro-sex, pro-boundary-crossing sexual politics, and works to open porn to a range of political and aesthetic interventions and social actors. From this perspective, CUM2CUT participants contribute to a larger sexual-social commons.

PORN INTO LIFE

What, then, is the *élan vital* of gay DIY porn that I have chased after in this chapter? Recall that for Bergson *élan vital* was less a solution to the problem of mechanism versus vitalism, but a new way of thinking materialism, of understanding matter as agentive. It wasn't an answer but a placeholder for the innate, ineffable creativity of matter. As he put it, "the 'vital principle' might indeed not explain much, but it is at least a sort of label affixed to our ignorance, so as to remind us of this occasionally, while mechanism invites us to ignore that ignorance."[42] Rather than view life as a predictable progression of the selfish interests of brute matter, Bergson understood evolutionary change as life's agentive response to a range of pressures and constraints: "The living being possesses a capacity for reaction, an activity of its own that allows it to resist brutal, purely physical forces. By this we do not want to say . . . that the soul is truly in a struggle with the forces of inorganic nature, but we maintain that forces do not behave totally the same in the presence of brute matter, and living matter. Up to a certain point, the effect is indeterminate."[43] The vitality of online gay DIY porn doesn't lie in the way it represents a better or more evolved porn, but in the way it opens up a creative immanence, the capacity to solicit the participation of publics, laterally or directly resist or elaborate normative pornographic conventions, to animate and enliven our pornographic imaginations and shared sexual cultures. Gay DIY porn moves bodies and desires, and makes good, however unevenly, on the promises participatory culture offers for democratic alternatives to the incorporation of everyday life, and of sex itself as an expanding and vital, even or especially if nonprocreative, practice of life. The light that emanates from the queer space of the screen, that touches bodies, is, like the ejaculate that arcs in response to some virtual world of desire, a form of matter, literally life-giving.

CODA

On Not Hooking Up

In John Cameron Mitchell's 2006 film *Shortbus,* Ceth (pronounced "Seth"), a willowy young model, navigates an indy queer salon/party/ orgy also called "Shortbus" in New York City. He has a mobile device with him, a "Yenta," that exclaims, "I've got a match for you!" when he nears Magnus, a tall, black potential match with a cool haircut. They look at each other and at their screens and chat about their stats. We don't know if Ceth and Magnus hook up, though there's plenty of sex in the film. In fact, *Shortbus* is centrally concerned with sex and the ways it supports or disorganizes coupled and communal intimacies. It focuses especially on the fraught relationship sex has to the couple form and, at the same time, the ways carnality offers a productively troubling route toward self-transformation and collective sociability. The film doesn't sidestep the hard work of intimacy, and yet it manages to be hopeful, even utopian. Couples go through the grinder: one breaks up, the other opens up to a third member, and no closure of any kind is provided.

Other kinds of coupling are represented as well, often graphically, even if, like Magnus or Shabbos Goy, a Jewish transsexual performance artist/shaman, they don't get quite as much screen time as Ceth with the model good looks or the whitebread couple he ends up with (the Jamies), or the tattooed, smiling hetero pair the film's central character, Sofia, watches from a couch in the orgy room. Still, John Cameron Mitchell's sensitivity in including a racially, morphologically, and otherwise diverse array of bodies and acts echoes the central characters'

123

hunger for difference and growth and supports a politically attuned queerness that celebrates the capaciousness of intimate forms.

This complex and fraught, if also hopeful, image of queer desire, and the forms latent to it, stands in contrast to Grindr success stories. Cameron's then-fanciful mobile PDA hookup device, the Yenta, was a prescient forerunner to Grindr. Released in 2009, Grindr is a smart phone app that promises connections—platonic, romantic, sexual, and otherwise—to men on the move. As I put it in chapter 3, the application updates gay cruising for the digital age. On Grindr's Web site one finds brief, and strangely desexualized, descriptions of the program, as well as a link to "Grindr Stories." While the app appears to be designed as a tool to hook up—find gay men nearby right now!—these stories deemphasize this quality, underscoring instead the ways casual sex is only one possible effect among others. A few stories describe how the app enabled men in remote or homophobic places to connect with one another and form communities. But most of the stories highlight Grindr as an accidental or awkward step toward something more real, a real relationship with soulmates, husbands, and life partners. Anthony from Toronto writes, for example, "I typically used Grindr to cure the onset of boredom, and hell, even hooked up using it. Never thought in a million years I would have met the love of my life on it! We've been together now for 1.5 years and probably gonna pop the question in the near future as well. I have to thank Grindr for making this union possible or I would have never met my soul mate!" Josh from Palm Springs also found the love of his life (at least for the last six months) on Grindr after on and off again use. Now that the couple has formed, "We've both deleted our Grindr apps, and no offense, but we don't ever plan on downloading them again!"

Users around the world have downloaded Grindr many millions of times. It and programs like it have become part of the texture of gay life, part of the media ecologies that shape our daily practices and desires, that transform how we think of ourselves and how we move through the world.[1] Grindr is among the media and technological forms, such as sociable robots, networked connectivity, and mobile devices that allow us, according to Sherry Turkle, to construct new ways of being "alone together," to feel close when and how we want. After many years of underscoring the promise of computers in helping us to connect in often playful ways to others or ourselves, Turkle strikes a more cautionary note in *Alone Together*. She focuses on the ways new media technologies and practices—such as cell phones and texting, or apps like Grindr—allow us to exercise control over our relationships, existing or incipient, and to tune out when we don't want to connect. Of course "making demands" is a practice tied to intimacy, care, and mutuality.[2] When we abdicate our culpability to intimates or even to strangers, we might experience a sense of control or freedom, but we are sacrificing what makes intimacy nourishing: the care and mutuality, and also the difficulties that help us to grow as ethical, relating persons. Turkle worries about the ways that we increasingly want space *and* closeness; but, often, what we do to maintain this sense of being alone together means that we can never feel close enough. She wryly notes the ways we are hurt by others' freedoms, by their distancing whenever (our) too close is too much (for them). We lament our solitude and resist (and resent) the work that comes with being together.

Grindr says it offers an easy-to-use alternative to other Web-based social networking or dating services because it doesn't require men to answer lengthy or invasive questions about their favorite bands, their psychological makeup, or even what they are really online for. Instead, as in the vernacular cultures that have emerged in the wake of texting, tweeting, and online cruising, information is narrowly telescoped: describe yourself in 140 characters or less. All of this, of course, is intended to make it easy to meet other men while otherwise engaged in our on-the-go lives. Yet, as with so many of the other promises I discuss in the book, these aspirations are cut through with failures. And these failures are generative of sociable forms that do not conform to the stated aims of Grindr, Inc., which tends to disappear sex (it's just about "meeting" other gay guys), or to the ostensible expectations of the men who populate the screens of one another's mobile devices (just looking for hookups). Failure underscores the uncaptured immanence of intimate virtualities, and how these virtualities take shape in things, in moments, events, the apps themselves, and the practice of browsing—things that do not look like what we usually mean by intimacy. With Grindr and other new media apps, "easy" isn't. Material limits drag on and also co-constitute the possibilities latent in Grindr, and in the affective and social structures that emerge in the wake of the failure to connect in the ways one hoped for.

MATERIAL BOYS LIVING IN AN (IM)MATERIAL WORLD

Grindr wants us to hook up, to channel our desires into chat, dates, relationships, sex, and networking. But something emerges in the space of everyday practice. It can't be this easy, and it's not. Firstly, there is an array of material constraints. These include the technical constraints of one's mobile device. The very ability to use the program is determined by the capacity of silicon to conduct electrical signals and the speed at which such signals travel. Batteries run out, especially if you check Grindr every few moments to refresh the grid of local men or respond to messages. When I used to cruise Grindr, my iPhone 3GS battery was exhausted after a couple of hours of use. And when, after a few years of drawing power from the grid, the phone dies for good, or when it's lost, it enters into a vast stream of technological waste. This mechanical dissolution can uncannily mirror the loss of intimacies—the phone numbers, photos, and memories that make these devices so meaningful to us. Then there's money, too: without a wi-fi connection, being online means using a data plan, and these plans have become increasingly stingy. Thus, while the program's boosters say that you can be on the move, the ideal location is likely a semi-private place, such as a cafe or bookstore with free wi-fi, where you can plug in, settle down, and browse (more on which below). So although the app is meant to untether men from their computers, using Grindr while on the move presents other challenges. One can't, and shouldn't, use it while driving, for instance (I've tried). And Grindr is useless on underground transportation because it requires either a satellite or wi-fi signal (good luck sending a note to the cute guy on the A train). Buses and trains can be good places to use the app, but then one has to worry about nosy neighbors while responding to a potential date's request for a picture of your junk. This can be challenging in a packed bus or if the person sitting next to you is looking over your shoulder. You have to hold your phone like a miniature lover, close to your chest in a protective, hunched embrace. The program will moreover disappoint those who had hoped for a calming, mechanical voice to guide them, step by step, to the nearest sexual encounter. It doesn't work quite like a GPS anyway—you can't just use it like radar to direct you to your object of desire: "turn right and arrive at your dick/destination."

Above all, there are material limits that have to do with embodiment and temporality. Grindr promises the ability to meet someone right away. But this pretty much never happens. You have to create a profile, identify people you might be interested in, contact them, engage in small talk, feel them out, find out what they're into, figure out if they're actually a troll trying to get you worked up, exchange pictures and locations. Then, if you're hooking up, for example, you might like to shower and change before meeting someone for the first time. If you're a really busy fella on the move, taking a bus, say, do you really have the time to arrange for a hookup on the way?

IMAGE LABOR

Men work hard to produce and manage their Grindr avatars. As I discussed earlier, the profile creation process is laden with affective demands and effects. There, I focused on anxiety, paranoia, and optimism as dominant modes that organize the experience of being black and gay online. Here, I'm interested more broadly in the forms of work that go into producing, promoting, and managing one's profile on a program such as Grindr, a sort of ongoing process of becoming[3] in which affective and other largely intangible forms of work matter a great deal to the erotic excitement that defines the app's appeal. Following Mark Coté and Jennifer Pybus, Sharif Mowlabocus underscores the role of affect in the social/sexual networking and commerce that take place on Web 2.0 sites such as Xtube.[4] Like XTube and other social networking applications, Grindr demands forms of work in which affect is the "binding, dynamic force which both animates [virtual] subjectivities and provides coherence to the networked relations."[5] In order to be connected with others, men have to carefully select the material they wish to share and how they wish to frame it. This decision-making process includes, among other things, the choice of how much of themselves, their fleshy embodiments, they wish to reveal. While Grindr does not permit nudity or other sexually explicit images, many users show some skin in closely cropped shots of their abs or chest. And many users choose to include images with their faces visible as well. But disclosing one's face might have undesirable effects. Whether in a small town or a big city, a face is personal, intimate—it risks being recognized by strangers on the street, or by office mates, judgmental friends, or a lover who might be checking things out, or checking up on you. Showing face means you're serious, but it also risks censure.

Creating a profile also requires brevity. "Fun," "Friendly," "Smart," "Muscles," "Swimmer's Build," "Yoga," "Sexy"? Most profile text becomes generic, almost meaningless, a problem I have seen many users overcome by simply excluding almost all text, including profile handles. They're blank. These blank Grindr profiles appear as a kind of pure image, an object-event that invites our gaze, interpretation, and interaction, yielding nothing concrete, only seductive possibility.

There's work involved in maintaining a profile, even a profile that refuses to perform the work of profiles. As my informant Redy put it in chapter 3, it's important to stay "fresh." The labor that goes into one's profile or being online isn't simply about creating a profile and then waiting to see what happens, or getting online, chatting with someone, and meeting. Rather, it enters one into a marketplace of desire, of sexual value and existing hierarchies (Leo Bersani famously challenged boosters of gay sex cultures for underplaying the brutally ranked competitiveness of cruising and sex publics). What you choose to disclose, and how, matters; you have to change a profile to stay interesting and relevant, to matter. Then there are the categories that can make or break your chances: size, age, race, among others. Showing too much or not enough or never updating anything can all risk failure—like a good Boy Scout, you always have to be prepared! There is, then, always the need to have images on hand, images that carefully present oneself in the best possible light, and images that might answer someone's demand to show more. And not disclosing these things, just like the refusal to share images of one's face, also endangers one's chances to connect. It is not enough to simply enter the space with a profile; there's a need to produce and hold on to the sexual/cultural capital you've accumulated with good grooming practices, trips to the gym, and carefully selected and rehearsed readymade examples of who you "really" are. So people update their pictures, delete accounts and make new ones, carefully curate images from the increasingly vast photographic archives most of us possess, come up with clever things to say, or say nothing at all. Men rework their profiles if they want to remain anonymous (as is often the case in small towns or urban neighborhoods dense with gay social networks), if they want to create a respectable image so they can find a tour guide in a city they are visiting, or if they're looking to hook up with someone for a long-term relationship, or just to trade pics and jerk off.

DOUCHEBAGS OF GRINDR

The image management of keeping it fresh isn't new or particular to Grindr. Many new technologies that promise simplicity and ease actually make us busier as we learn to use them to organize our lives, prepare the perfect meal, or meet the perfect mate. And, as I've already pointed out, Grindr also refracts earlier cultural practices such as cruising or the sexually explicit chat made possible by IRC and Web portals like Gay.com. But it also produces new ones. Douchebags of Grindr is a blog containing screenshots of Grindr "douchebags," people whose profiles violate others' ethical or aesthetic sensibilities. The site responds to the insensitive, politically incorrect, or just plain fucked up profile texts that the relative anonymity of the app and the need for brevity in profiles inevitably produce. Douchebags of Grindr makes these snafus public. Its "name and shame" methods ostensibly serve as an ethical calling out of the many forms of social and sexual exclusion men express in their profiles. Posts to the site are tagged with words that are anathema to the apolitical leanings of homonorms: "racism," "ageism," "body nazi," "self-loathing," and "femmephobia" (this last tag is ironic given the misogynistic epithet from which the site derives its name). Then there are specific terms new to Grindr publics like "blockophiles" (people who take pleasure in blocking other profiles) and "mezzy," which, as best as I can make out, is a corruption of "messy" often applied to men whose profile texts are rife with grammatical errors. However, the douchebags who are called out, and some of their friends, view the site as a vengeful effort to humiliate and silence people who are just expressing their "personal preferences"; they view those who submit to the site as scorned losers.[6] And, in fact, the comments that discuss profiles often veer into "troll" territory, themselves using provocative speech to disrupt a comment thread or goad others into indignant responses. The logic of the site is thus fraught with incoherencies. It responds to some men on Grindr in order to shame them, while often intolerantly decrying the various forms of intolerance these men's profiles express. Douchebags of Grindr reframes the app's instrumental aspirations. People who post there are not only using Grindr to hook up, chat, or network; they are scanning the grid, checking people out, and reflecting on the boundaries of what makes a gay public. They are attuned to the politics and potentialities of queer sociability and by collecting, posting, and commenting on "douches" they help to constitute other kinds of publics (of gay politics or trolling) and practices, ones that operate alongside gay networks of desire, or the parallel reality that is gay cruising, while simultaneously resisting the exclusionary logics that shape these networks and realities.

Douchebags of Grindr thus reflects the generativity of cultural forms; showing how Grindr is much more than an application men use to hook up. Men do hook up, of course, but they also check in, check up on people, and browse. They hook up, or not.

"Remediation," a term developed by Jay Bolter and Richard Grusin, helps make sense of what Grindr does.[7] Remediation describes processes by which earlier and existing media forms are repurposed, and the ways attendant social and cultural forms are likewise reworked. It describes the ways technologies, texts, or socialities can be recombined into new material and semiotic assemblages. It emphasizes how media are not merely taken for granted things, or, in the case of Grindr, the means by which one might actualize one's desires. Media always have histories; media always remediate. As Mary Gray parses Bolter and Grusin's argument, "New media circulate old stories entwining or commingling aesthetics of media forms to keep some narratives and forms of storytelling prioritized over others."[8] Eugene Thacker uses Bolter and Grusin's insights to think through the body's remediation, the ways in which it is caught between "the poles of immediacy and hypermediacy, the 'body itself' and the body enframed by sets of discourses (social, political, scientific)."[9] In the case of Grindr, the app draws on and reworks earlier real-time interactive technologies such as telephones or online chat rooms, as well as the features of social networking sites, to enable men to connect with one another through their mobile devices. Like earlier media technologies, it promises real-time connections, including sex, while also being situated within a larger media-saturated world; even in the app, one has to navigate the images of profiles, ads, and multiple screens as one clicks through the different layers of a profile to learn more about someone or to chat. Remediation also puts into relief the ways social forms like cruising, which combines proximity, spare gestures, and hierarchies of exclusion, are both reproduced in and through new media technologies and assembled or expressed in new ways. For example, online, conditions of anonymity and exposure allow men to express their ageist or racist views with relative impunity, while Douchebags of Grindr tries to shame them for doing so. Finally, the technophobic and technophilic relations to technologies are themselves remediated. Grindr is at once celebrated for allowing men to find other men nearby, and critiqued for producing anxiety as men feel subjected to surveillance (by their neighbors or boyfriends) or for narrowing gay sociality to the space of screens in which proximate men are laid out on a grid, available for one's perusal like an endless row of nearly indistinguishable cereal boxes at the supermarket.

FIGURE 6.1. Matteo, Douchebag?

Matteo's Grindr profile is tagged with "arrogant" and "racism." His profile text reads: "Not into spice or rice. Go subscribe to National Geographic, make a list of places you'll never get to visit. Add to that list me." Like other profiles identified as arrogant, Matteo's doucheyness is tied to his inflated sense of himself and the corresponding lack of self-awareness about the kind of effects his arrogance might produce in others. His arrogance also takes shape as a cruel, racist dismissal of Latinos and Asians (spice and rice). But there's also a kind of bitchy performativity here that confuses things. Matteo combines the racist dismissal of Latinos and Asians with a reference to *National Geographic,* a kind of touchstone for colonial fantasies of difference. This reference communicates a bit of class-inflected shade: you're never going to visit these places because you're poor. I'm one of those places and therefore out of your league. The comments that respond to Matteo's profile are likewise confused, at once challenging Matteo's self-important racism and reproducing stereotyped ideas about racial, sexual, cultural difference. One respondent, Kimmois, for example, adds "Douchebag" to a list of places he doesn't want to go: "Chechnya, Kabul, Rwanda, Mogadishu, Congo, Caracas, Douchebag." Another commenter, BB, does something similar: "one way ticket to Douchebagistan pls, this dude needs it so much." Matteo and his detractors seem to engage in a specifically gay mode of critique: the "read," an attitude or form of speech that insults. Does this mean that Matteo's a douchebag? Are they?

"Are you him??" is the handle of a beefy young man in a hoodie, smiling with his hands in a thumbs-up position. His profile text reads: "Looking for him. R u him?? WHITES ONLY!! All blacks, keep moving cuz I ain't interested unless you can prove not all blacks are the exact same mkay?" His profile is tagged "racism" and the comments revel in identifying his physical flaws. o rly says, "It's one thing to be racist, but to be racist when you're fat and ugly is simply unacceptable. Hope this one enjoys being single for eternity." While BB reads Are you him?? thusly: "I'd be amused if he was looking for Her on grindr, but he would have even less chances with gurls even compared to sick, desperate, borderline myopic afro people who might have somehow missed all the fat and hypocrisy he has to offer."

The name and shame tactics themselves are here even more obviously douchey. They move away from an ethical critique of practices of exclusion and instead focus on a douche's physical or grammatical flaws. I tried to strike a balance of my own when I responded to a thread of comments about BI MASC, dubbed "Polite douche" by the site's administrator. BI MASC's profile text read, "sorry but only into white: successful E commerce owner. Often told I'm masculine, intelligent, witty, discrete, polite, honest, grounded." Weighing in on whether or not BI MASC's expression of a racial preference is racist,

Jgay wrote, "The racial preference argument is just as strong as our gay argument. If we didn't have a preference to certain characteristics solely belonging to a certain race, then why do we have a preference for men at all?" I responded, like a good anthropologist, I think:

> JGay, don't be a simpleton. What you are basically saying is that racial preferences and homosexuality are simply a matter of individual taste. We don't exist in a vacuum and our tastes, desires, and the like aren't simply things we put on like a pair of socks. They are cultural. The tricky part is how we come to view preferences as natural and personal rather than as the effects of our cultural upbringing, larger societal mores, and many deeply engrained prejudices. Have you stopped to ask yourself why SO MANY people have the same "preferences"? What happens when you scratch the surface of "no chocolate/no rice, sorry just a preference"? Why don't people want to be with men of color? Well, because they don't find them attractive. Why don't they find them attractive? I mean, come on, it's not like all Blacks, Latinos, or Asians come in one shape or size, right? But when someone says no to an entire group, he's saying I don't find ANY of you attractive, because you're all the same. This idea, that all members of a racial group are the same, is by definition racist because it fails to recognize the incredible diversity within racial groupings.

Browsing Douchebags of Grindr, I got caught up in the douchebaggery. I wanted to intervene decisively. But in doing so, was I missing the point? The comments pages on the site don't settle debates about the ethics of "preferences," racism, or femmephobia. They remediate them, along with the intimate possibilities the often insulting back and forth imagine or delimit (fat boys shouldn't be racist, self-identified masculine men are insecure bottoms). The site and the commenters also illustrate the ways that other practices constellate around the instrumentalist promise of the app. People are going on Grindr to see who's online, to see who's hot and whose douchey, and some are collecting or curating an archive of douchebaggery, contesting the logic of individual preferences or the easy hookup.

In many ways, trolling Grindr is easier than using it to hook up. Or rather, it operates as a kind of supplemental practice: cruising for sexual partners, one also cruises for something else. Put differently, cruising has become multiplied—men may be looking for hookups, friends, or networking, but they're also looking for douchebags. They're not just looking for people they're interested in, but for people who are engaging in practices considered to be harmful to the larger imagined community of gay people.

Trolling Grindr functions as a refusal to play by the rules of the game, a refusal to adhere to the logic and discourse of hooking up. At the most general level, trolling is about provocation and trying to get a rise out of people. It's a refusal to play nice. Douchebags of Grindr curiously performs this role, refusing to let the douchebaggery of some of the men who use Grindr go without critique. But is this really a public service aimed at contesting the exclusionary language men use when they're on the hunt for sex and connection or is it an expression of queer anti-sociality, more evidence that "communities" are not communitarian? Are any of the douchebags profiled on the site more than modestly inconvenienced, if they know about the site at all? If the site is intended to diminish racism, ageism, or homophobia, then how do we understand the trolling in the comments' section that seems to make up the site's most lively aspect? At the very least the site helps to interrupt the instrumental claims of the app's makers: hooking up isn't easy, especially if vigilant trolls are working hard to shame guys on the move looking for a good time. Douchebags of Grindr archives the vulnerability of going online, of looking for something but not getting it, or for saying what you want and getting shamed for it.

ON THE IMMANENCE OF BROWSING

I personally prefer an instrumental approach to online cruising. Over the years of working and playing in online queer publics, I developed a series of practices to avoid spending long periods online when research bled into something else. I set time limits if I was on the hunt (hour max), or, if I was soliciting the interest of potential playmates or informants, I would often log into a program and then leave to walk my dog, responding to messages when I returned. I tried to balance clarity with openness in my profiles: "looking for fun and friendship," "looking for real connections." I never lied about my age or my weight. And I only got online if I knew what I was looking for: a quick chat, an answer to a question about a new city, or sex. I had other rules, too: face pics were a must; no one on the down low or who wasn't out; no Republicans; no one who didn't know what they wanted; no endless back and forth; and if sex was on the table, then there needed to be a text or a phone call after the first few exchanges. After ten years of being online, I didn't want to "waste" more time. Browsing was not something I liked to do. But for others, browsing is precisely the point of going online.

Browsing is an embodied, durational practice that belongs to an alternative logic of consumption that emphasizes the pleasure of look-ing rather than the pleasure of having or getting. People go online not knowing what they want. They surf the Net to hang out or be alone together. To see what's going on and who else is online. To check on their friends or exes. Browsing invites the serendipitous or chance event. "I don't know what I want or what I'm looking for, but maybe I'll know it if I see it." Like Douchebags of Grindr, browsing interrupts the stated purpose of Grindr, but unlike Douchebags, it has even less discernible aims. On the surface, it seems to adhere to the instrumental logic of Grindr's meat market insofar as the visual and gestural practices that shape it reflect some preexisting, if only partially articulated, structure of desire. You do not look at or chat with anyone, but with someone you have some latent or not fully formed interest in. But browsing's object is elusive; the pleasure is in the more or less aimless search.[10]

Browsing is something you do to enjoy being in the flow of desire rather than trying to satiate it. It is oriented toward possibili-ties. On Grindr, to really get a full sense of the possibilities (romantic, sexual, and otherwise) available, you have to contact a lot of people, and respond to a lot of messages. You have to be willing to let the small talk play out, to feel out latent interests or connections.

Browsing is optimistically open to the chance of success, with-out settling on what success might look or feel like. It could be a random Tuesday night threeway, a coffee, massage, or something else you haven't thought of yet. Or, it ignores success altogether. After all, no actual "successfully realized" contact can match the intimate scenes one imagines; to find those scenes concretized would run the risk of snuffing out the desire that animates them. It is the immanence, the force of potential, of some thing that is not knowable in advance, that is key to the enjoyment of browsing. Dwelling in this zone of latent discovery can for some be a good deal more enjoyable than actualizing anything. Browsing is thus a real event unto itself; and it is virtual, productive of lags, deferrals, and uncertain socialities.

For most of us, approaching intimacy in this way might be frustrating in its refusal to embrace instrumentalist approaches in which feeling connected or having sex results from a prescription dutifully followed, tasks checked off on the path to erotic or romantic success. Browsing can be like holding a world in your hands. Refusing determinist narratives of progression or ease, this world contains multitudes: casual sex, unlikely arrangements of kin, disappointments, fleeting and fiercely enduring attachments. Browsing possesses a power that is also an invitation; the queerspace of the screen summons us to imagine a more expansive array of potential modes of relating. These virtual intimacies, the constellation of latent capacities and routes that might be actualized, or not, serve as reminders that the generativity of queer socialities has not been exhausted, and that we cannot know in advance or for certain what forms our intimacies with ourselves or others might take.

Notes

INTRODUCTION

1. Gilles Deleuze, "Immanence: A Life," in *Pure Immanence: Essays on a Life,* trans. Anne Boyman (New York: Zone Books, 2001), 31.

2. Lauren Berlant, "Intimacy: A Special Issue," in *Intimacy,* ed. Lauren Berlant (Chicago: University of Chicago Press, 2000), 1.

3. For a history of religious opposition to interracial and same-sex marriage, see George Chauncey, *Why Marriage?: The History Shaping Today's Debate Over Gay Equality* (New York: Basic Books, 2005). For the usefulness and limits of the analogy between miscegenation and gay marriage, see especially pages 157–65.

4. Gayle Rubin, "Thinking Sex: Notes for a Radical Theory of the Politics of Sexuality," in *The Lesbian and Gay Studies Reader,* ed. Henry Abelove, Michéle Aina Barana, and David Halperin (New York: Routledge, 1993), 3–44.

5. Sara Ahmed, *The Cultural Politics of Emotion* (New York: Routledge, 2004), 80n2.

6. Manuel Castells, *The Power of Identity* (Malden, MA: Blackwell, 2004).

7. Then there are also the many ways the promise of cyberspace has been drawn into capitalism's grasp, although this is not a focus of this book. As Jonathan Zittrain makes clear in his book, *The Future of the Internet and How to Stop It,* the Internet is returning to models of gated communities (like AOL and Facebook), and the generative and collaborative sharing represented by the Free and Open Source software movement, by filesharing, or the now ubiquitous Wikipedia are being eclipsed by tethered proprietary devices (Apple's iPhones, for example) that can be modified only by the corporate

manufacturer or its partners. These devices as well as Web 2.0 platforms such as Facebook not only restrict the abilities of users to create changes in the software but also increasingly engage in various forms of surveillance and data mining among its users. See Zittrain, *The Future of the Internet and How to Stop It* (New Haven: Yale University Press, 2008). The book is also available for free under a Creative Commons License; it can be downloaded here: http://futureoftheinternet.org/download.

8. Kathleen Stewart, "On the Politics of Cultural Theory: A Case for 'Contaminated' Critique," *Social Research* 58, no. 2 (1991): 395–412.

9. Samuel Delany, *Times Square Red, Times Square Blue* (New York: New York University Press, 1999), 111.

10. See Michael Warner, *The Trouble with Normal: Sex, Politics, and the Ethics of Queer Life* (New York: The Free Press, 1999) and the film *Gay Sex in the '70s* (Joseph Lovett, dir., 2005).

11. Martin Meeker, *Contacts Desired: Gay and Lesbian Communications and Community, 1940s–1970s* (Chicago: University of Chicago Press, 2006), 1.

12. Ibid,, 2.

13. Ibid., 3.

14. Alexander Galloway, "Networks," in *Critical Terms for Media Studies,* ed. W. J. T. Mitchell and Mark Hansen (Chicago: University of Chicago Press, 2010), 283.

15. Ibid.

16. Marnia Robinson and Gary Wilson, "Straight Men, Gay Porn' and Other Brain Map Mysteries," *Psychology Today,* February 3, 2010, http://www.psychologytoday.com/blog/cupids-poisoned-arrow/201002/straight-men-gay-porn-and-other-brain-map-mysteries; accessed May 19, 2011.

17. Gilles Deleuze, "Immanence: A Life," 31.

18. See Kathleen Stewart, "Weak Theory in an Unfinished World," *Journal of Folklore Research* 45, no. 1 (2008): 71–82; and *Ordinary Affects* (Durham: Duke University Press, 2007).

19. Rob Shields, *The Virtual* (New York: Routledge, 2003).

20. Among others, see George Chauncey, *Gay New York: Gender, Urban Culture, and the Making of the Gay Male World: 1890–1940* (New York: Basic Books, 1994); John D'Emilio and Estelle B. Freedman, *Intimate Matters: A History of Sexuality in America* (New York: Harper and Row, 1988), and the essays in David Higgs, ed., *Queer Sites: Gay Urban Histories Since 1600* (New York: Routledge, 1999).

21. Brian Massumi, *Parables for the Virtual: Movement, Affect, Sensation* (Durham: Duke University Press, 2002).

22. Psychoanalysis, for example, which has inspired me in many ways, but does not centrally figure in this book, has robust conceptions of fantasy and haunting that resonate with my own use of virtuality.

23. Lauren Berlant, *Cruel Optimism* (Durham: Duke University Press, 2011).

24. Jodi Dean, *Democracy and Other Neoliberal Fantasies: Communicative Capitalism and Left Politics* (Durham: Duke University Press, 2009).

25. Lisa Duggan, *The Twilight of Equality: Neoliberalism, Cultural Politics, and the Attack on Democracy* (Boston: Beacon Press, 2003).

26. Homonationalism describes the ways nationalist ideologies recruit homosexuality into their image of "progressive" and "democratic" freedoms; the fact that gays are not stoned or are permitted some of the rights of their hetero compatriots operates as an alibi for imperialist projects and the permanent "war on terror." See Jasbir Puar, *Terrorist Assemblages: Homonationalism in Queer Times* (Durham: Duke University Press, 2007).

27. This homonationalism is evident in recent debates about the relationship between homosexuality and broader global politics. For example, Israeli leaders, Toronto's mayor Rob Ford, and porn mogul Michael Lucas have scolded the activist group Queers Against Israeli Apartheid for misrecognizing their political objects. Sexual politics, the former argue, is not geopolitics. Of course long histories of queer political engagements give the lie to these arguments, whether we think of anticensorship work, support for the end of American apartheid (past and present), health care, or the ways progressive left queers vocally objected to the illegal invasion of Iraq.

28. Jason Pine, *The Art of Making Do in Naples* (Minneapolis: University of Minnesota Press, 2012).

29. See Judith Halberstam, *In a Queer Time and Place: Transgender Bodies, Subcultural Lives* (New York: New York University Press, 2005).

30. Henry Jenkins, *Convergence Culture: Where Old and New Media Collide* (New York: New York University Press, 2006).

31. Melissa Gregg, "A Mundane Voice," *Cultural Studies* 18, no. 2/3 (2004): 364.

32. Imgoen Tyler and Elena Loizidou, "The Promise of Lauren Berlant," *Cultural Values* 4, no. 3 (2000): 505.

CHAPTER ONE. THE VIRTUAL LIFE OF SEX IN PUBLIC

1. Georges Bataille, *The Tears of Eros,* trans. Peter Connor (San Francisco: City Lights Books, 1989), 67.

2. See Lauren Berlant's introduction in *The Female Complaint: The Unfinished Business of Sentimentality in American Culture* (Durham: Duke University Press, 2008), 2, where she focuses, in part, on the ways "a sentimental account of the social world as an affective space where people ought to be legitimated because they have feelings and because there is an intelligence in what they feel that *knows* something about the world that, if it were listened to, could make things better."

3. In *Virtually Normal* (New York: Vintage, 1996), Andrew Sullivan challenged both established models of gay politics and state policies that would deny gays and lesbians the right to marriage and military service. See

Michael Warner's impassioned, and equally polemical, response to Sullivan, *The Trouble with Normal: Sex, Politics, and the Ethics of Queer Life* (New York: The Free Press, 1999) in which he argues that the efforts of Sullivan and others to achieve mainstream acceptance actually function to intensify a politics of sexual shame directed at and internalized by queer cultures. See also Urvashi Vaid's important examination of the mainstreaming of gay and lesbian rights in *Virtual Equality* (New York: Anchor Books, 1995). Importantly, Sullivan's use of "virtual" emphasized the ways gay people were practically normal, while Vaid's analysis highlighted the ways queers had not achieved social or political recognition.

4. Steven Saylor, "Amethyst, Texas," in *Hometowns: Gay Men Write About Where They Belong,* ed. John Preston (New York: Plume, 1992), 122.

5. Esther Milne, "Email and Epistolary Technologies: Presence, Intimacy, Disembodiment," *Fibreculture,* no. 2 (2003); journal.fibreculture.org/issue2/issue2_milne.html.

6. KXAN News, "Sex, Parks, and Videotape," February 7, 2006; www.kxan.com/Global/story.asp?S=4464515.

7. Ibid.

8. See George Chauncey, *Gay New York: Gender, Urban Culture, and the Making of the Gay Male World 1890–1940* (New York: Basic Books); Neil Miller, *Sex Crime Panic: A Journey into the Paranoid Heart of the 1950s* (Los Angeles: Alyson Publications, 2002); William Leap, ed., *Public Sex/Gay Space* (New York: Columbia University Press, 1999); and Dangerous Bedfellows, eds., *Policing Public Sex: Queer Politics and the Future of AIDS Activism* (Boston: South End Press, 1996).

9. Though I do not discuss it in the following section, *TCAP* generated at least one suicide. A Texas county prosecutor killed himself after *TCAP* appeared at his house with a SWAT team.

10. KXAN, "Sex."

11. Editorial, "Pease Park is for All," *Austin American-Statesman,* June 22, 1996.

12. KXAN, "Sex."

13. Laud Humphreys, "Tearoom Trade," in *Public Sex/Gay Space,* ed. William Leap (New York: Columbia University Press, 1999 [1970]), 29–54.

14. Brian Ross, "Foley's IM Exchange with Underage Page," September 29, 2006; abcnews.go.com/WNT/BrianRoss/Story?id=2509586&page=3.

15. An expert on child sex laws, Foley's online communications and face-to-face liaisons carefully followed the letter of the laws he had helped draft.

16. Technically, the show and Perverted Justice use the term *predator* rather than pedophile; the former has an interest in underage partners, while the latter preys on prepubescent children. Yet, there is frequent slippage

between these two terms, as evidenced in an interview Mark Foley gave a year before his resignation on an MSNBC program in which he praised the work Perverted Justice and TCAP were doing to stop the sexual victimization of children online.

17. Linda Williams, *Hard Core: Power, Pleasure, and "The Frenzy of the Visible"* (Berkeley: University of California Press, 1989).

18. Chris Hansen, "Expensive Home Rich with Potential Predators," July 26, 2007; www.msnbc.msn.com/id/19961209/page/2/.

19. I am inspired here by Judith Halberstam's discussion of failure in *The Queer Art of Failure* (Durham: Duke University Press, 2011), 3–5.

CHAPTER TWO. INTIMACIES IN THE MULTI(PLAYER)VERSE

1. Scientists, at least some of them, take the notion of the multiverse seriously too—there are several competing theories, including "bubble theory," "the many worlds," and "string theory"—although scientific views on multiple universes aren't within the scope of this chapter.

2. Gameplay is largely organized around "questing," adventures where one battles monsters (or "mobs" for "mobile objects"), acquires goods (from gold to herbs), and develops skills (enchanting, leatherworking, tailoring). The objective of questing is less to reach the end of the game (there isn't strictly an end; more on this below) than to cultivate a meaningful life in the game world, a process that involves, essentially, becoming more powerful by gaining more experience and goods, and through engaging in forms of (largely) responsible sociability with others.

When players first download the game, they select a server—the combination of software and hardware that allows users to connect remotely over a network. In the case of *WoW* and other MMOGs, servers are owned and hosted by the company that has created the game, in this case, Blizzard Entertainment. In *WoW,* servers are referred to as "realms," and each realm contains a copy of the game world (a literalization of the notion of the multiverse). While there are millions of *WoW* users, they can't all be in the same place at the same time, even virtually. There are therefore many realms because of the technical limitations that arise when trying to host more than a few thousand players on the same server at the same time. Players can interact with all the other players on their server, but not across servers. As well, players can move between servers only under special circumstances. Finally, while the world on each server is the same, they do differ in regard to the kinds of play they afford. There are two main realm types, Normal, or Player versus Environment (PvE), in which players focus on working within and against the game environment through quests and fighting monsters or "mobs." The other realm type is Player versus Player (PvP), in which there is ongoing conflict between factions. In these realms, players of differing factions can attack one another, adding an element of danger, as well as making some of the game content more challenging to accomplish. Finally, there are also Role-playing (RP) servers that feature either PvE or PvP gaming content. The key distinction in PvP servers is that gamers must speak and behave as their character would, that is, they engage in fantasy historical role play.

3. Bartle, in Edward Castronova, *Synthetic Worlds: The Business and Culture of Online Games* (Chicago: University of Chicago Press, 2005), 72.

4. Race in the game refers to one of the now fourteen races available for game play, including humans, dwarves, night elves, and orcs among others. Class refers to the type of adventurer a player becomes; mage, priest, warrior, hunter, rogue, and so on. One's racial choice also determines the available classes. Blood Elves for example can be hunters but not shamans. The racial politics of the game are evident in two other ways. First, players are able to select from a range of hues for some in game races; but these choices don't, for example, enable a player to apply Asian or black features. Second, and more problematically, several *WoW* races are clearly racialized. Trolls, for example, are a mashup of African diasporic peoples; they speak with Jamaican accents, yet talk about voodoo and practice the Brazilian dance/ martial art *capoeria*. The Tauren, a race of minotaur-like creatures, likewise condense a range of stereotypes about indigenous peoples; they greet others with a solemnly inflected "How," live in longhouses, and articulate a noble but "primitive" respect for the natural world.

5. Tom Boellstorff, *Coming of Age in Second Life: An Anthropologist Explores the Virtually Human* (Princeton: Princeton University Press, 2008), 102.

6. See T. L. Taylor for a historical discussion that situates MMOGS in the larger histories of multiuser "persistent environments" in *Play Between Worlds: Exploring Online Game Culture* (Cambridge: MIT Press, 2006), 21–28.

7. Anne Allison describes how designer Tajiri Satoshi challenged dominant trends in game design for players to only compete or battle one another by conceiving of another model of connection between players: cooperative trading. Eleven of the total 151 original Pokémon on the original Game Boy console could only be acquired through connecting a cable to another gamer's console. Anne Allison, *Millennial Monsters: Japanese Toys and the Global Imagination* (Berkeley: University of California Press, 2006), 201.

8. The two essential classes, for instance, are "tanks," usually warriors or other well-armored, heavy damage-dealing classes, who serve as the main frontal attack of a group, and "healers," usually priests who keep tanks and other players alive as they struggle to defeat the tougher-than-average creatures found in dungeons. These classes are so in demand that some players sell their services for in-game gold, agreeing to participate in a group only on the basis of payment, a participation clearly representative of a transactional approach to collaboration.

9. See, as well, Taylor's discussion of instrumental play and power gamers, *Play Between Worlds,* chapter 3.

10. Lauren Berlant, in Nigel Thrift, *Non-Representational Theory* (New York: Routledge, 2008), 214.

11. For an excellent discussion of intimacy conceived as "contact and encounter" and how these intimacies are impacted by neoliberal development, see Samuel Delany, *Times Square Red, Times Square Blue* (New York: New York University Press, 1999).

12. Interestingly, some long-term gamers are completely unfamiliar with this phenomenon. At a 2008 conference on virtual worlds at the University of California at Irvine, a scholar and *WoW* gamer of four years claimed she had never known anyone to engage in in-game intimacies beyond the scope of friendship or the instrumental intimacies I described above. Immediately, though, another conference participant chimed in, "Oh no, it happens all the time. We've had big scandals about this in our guild."

13. Daniel Miller and Don Slater, "Relationships," in *The Anthropology of Media,* ed. Kelly Askew and Riachard R. Wilk (Oxford: Blackwell, 2002), 187.

14. See Esther Milne, "Email and Epistolary Technologies: Presence, Intimacy, Disembodiment," journal.fibreculture.org/issue2/issue2_milne.html. Milne argues that disembodiment is paradoxically necessary to certain, intense modes of intimacy. The experience of being apart, she says, whether from oneself or from another, enables "a fantasy of bodily proximity or presence." And this fantasy, as it is activated in Milne's study through letters, postcards, and e-mail, has a charge that other forms of intimacy, including face-to-face intimacy, might not produce.

15. BBC News, "Gay Rights Win in Warcraft World," February 13, 2006. news.bbc.co.uk/1/hi/technology/4700754.stm; accessed December 8, 2012.

16. John Armstrong, *Conditions of Love: The Philosophy of Intimacy* (New York: Norton, 2003), 50.

17. Gregory M. Lamb, "Are Multiplayer Online Games More Addictive?" *USA Today,* October 12, 2005. www.usatoday.com/tech/gaming/2005-10-12-mmorpgs-addictive_x.htm; accessed December 8, 2012.

18. Allison, *Millennial Monsters,* 85.

19. See, for example, MSNBC, "Why Are Geeks the New Chic?" December 12, 2007. www.msnbc.msn.com/id/22219377/; and the *New York Times,* "The Alpha Geeks," May 22, 2008. www.nytimes.com/2008/05/23/opinion/23brooks.html?ref=opinion.

20. Allison, *Millennial Monsters,* 72–73 and 84–85.

21. Citing a study on Japanese consumer trends in which users were asked to imagine their "dream houses," Allison describes how the imaginary dwellings, which were clearly intended to be occupied by one person and their things, indicated a desire to "protect one's own space without interfering

with others." Researchers found these solitary, but often very bright, spaces "autistic." Allison, *Millennial Monsters,* 88.

22. Players will sometimes create low-level avatars on an opposing faction to harass members of that faction.

23. See Taylor, *Play Between Worlds,* especially chapter 1; and Lori Kendall, *Hanging Out in the Virtual Pub* (Berkeley: University of California Press, 2002).

24. See Allison, *Millennial Monsters,* especially chapter 3; and John and Jean Comaroff, *Millennial Capitalism and the Culture of Neoliberalism* (Durham: Duke University Press, 2001).

25. Here, I borrow liberally from José Esteban Muñoz' discussion in his essay, "Cruising the Toilet," *GLQ* 13, nos. 2–3 (2007): 353–67.

26. Agamben, in Muñoz, "Cruising the Toilet," 360.

27. Steven Shaviro, "Interstitial Life: Novelty and Double Causality in Kant, Whitehead, and Deleuze." www.dhalgren.com/Othertexts/New.pdf; accessed March 18, 2012.

CHAPTER THREE. FEELING BLACK AND BLUE

1. Shaka McGlotten, "Virtual Intimacies: Love, Addiction, and Identity @ The Matrix," in *Queer Online: Media Technology and Society,* ed. Kate O'Riordan and David Phillips (New York: Peter Lang, 2007), 123–37; Shaka McGlotten "Ordinary Intersections: Speculations on Difference, Justice, and Utopia in Black Queer Life," *Transforming Anthropology* 20, no. 1 (2012): 45–66.

2. See José Esteban Muñoz's Blochian-inspired discussion of futurity in *Cruising Utopia: The Then and There of Queer Futurity* (New York: New York University Press, 2009).

3. I am, however, still very sympathetic to some of these utopian or optimistic impulses. See especially Sherry Turkle, *Life on the Screen: Identity in the Age of the Internet* (New York: Simon and Schuster, 1995); Allucquére Rosanne Stone, *The War of Desire and Technology at the Close of the Mechanical Age* (Cambridge: MIT Press, 1995).

4. For a handful of examples, see Beth E. Kolko, Lisa Nakamura, and Gilbert B. Rodman, eds., *Race in Cyberspace* (New York: Routledge, 1999); Lisa Nakamura, *Cybertypes: Race, Ethnicity, and Identity on the Internet* (New York: Routledge, 2002) and *Digitizing Race: Visual Cultures of the Internet* (Minneapolis: University of Minnesota Press, 2008); Cameron Bailey, "Virtual Skin: Articulating Race in Cyberspace," in *Immersed in Technology: Art and Virtual Environments,* ed. Mary Ann Moser and Douglas MacLeod (Cambridge: MIT Press, 1996), 29–49; Andil Gosine, "Brown to Blonde at Gay.com: Passing White in Queer Cyberspace" in *Queer Online: Media Technology and Sexuality,* ed. Kate O'Riordan and David Phillips (New York: Peter Lang, 2007), 139–53; Shaka McGlotten "Ordinary Intersections."

5. Dwight McBride, "It's a White Man's World," in *Why I Hate Abercrombie and Fitch* (New York: New York University Press, 2005), 88–131. In his social history, Kai Wright occasionally addresses the degree to which young gay men of color use online spaces to connect in his excellent *Drifting Toward Love: Black, Brown, Gay, and Coming of Age on the Streets of New York* (Boston: Beacon Press, 2008).

6. Nigel Thrift, *Non-Representational Theory: Space | Politics | Affect* (New York: Routledge, 2008); Ben Anderson and John Wylie, "On Geography and Materiality" *Environment and Planning A* 41 (2009): 318–35.

7. Among others, see Lauren Berlant, "Intimacy: A Special Issue," in *The Female Complaint: The Unfinished Business of Sentimentality in American Culture* (Durham: Duke University Press, 2008); Eve Sedgwick, *Touching Feeling: Affect, Performativity, Pedagogy* (Durham: Duke University Press, 2003); Ann Cvetkovich, *An Archive of Feelings: Trauma, Sexuality, and Lesbian Public Cultures* (Durham: Duke University Press, 2003); Neville Hoad, *African Intimacies: Race, Homosexuality, and Globalization* (Minneapolis: University of Minnesota Press, 2007); and Kathleen Stewart, *Ordinary Affects* (Durham: Duke University Press, 2007).

8. See the "Feel Tank Manifesto." http://feeltankchicago.net/; accessed June 17, 2010.

9. David Eng and David Kazanjian, eds., *Loss: The Politics of Mourning* (Berkeley: University of California Press, 2002); Avery Gordon, *Ghostly Matters: Haunting in the Sociological Imagination* (Minneapolis: University of Minnesota Press, 1997); Sharon Holland, *Raising the Dead: Readings in Death and (Black) Subjectivity* (Durham: Duke University Press, 2000).

10. For one overview of this work, see Hayden Lorimer, "Cultural Geography: The Busyness of Being More-Than-Representational," *Progress in Human Geography* 29, no. 1 (2005): 83–94.

11. Eric Shouse, "Feeling, Emotion, Affect," *M/C Journal* 8, no. 6 (2005). http://journal.media-culture.org.au/0512/03-*shouse*.php; accessed June 17, 2010.

12. Brian Massumi, *Parables for the Virtual: Movement, Affect, Sensation* (Durham: Duke University Press, 2002).

13. Phillip Fisher, *The Vehement Passions* (Princeton: Princeton University Press, 2002).

14. See Celeste Henery, *The Balance of Souls: Self-Making and Mental Wellness in the Lives of Aging Black Women in Brazil* (PhD diss, University of Texas at Austin, 2010).

15. Sianne Ngai, "Animatedness," in *Ugly Feelings* (Cambridge: Harvard University Press 2005), 93.

16. In E. Patrick Johnson, *Appropriating Blackness: Performance and the Politics of Authenticity* (Durham: Duke University Press, 2003), 23.

17. Ibid.

18. Ibid., 2.

19. Ibid., 8. See also John L. Jackson Jr., *Real Black: Adventures in Racial Sincerity* (Durham: Duke University Press, 2005).

20. Donna Haraway, *Modest_Witness@SecondMillenium. FemaleMan_ Meets_OncoMouse: Feminism and Technoscience* (New York: Routledge, 1997), 213.

21. Fred Moten, "Black Mo'nin'" in *Loss: The Politics of Mourning,* 59–76.

22. Simon Critchley, "Being and Time Part 5: Anxiety." http://www. guardian.co.uk/commentisfree/belief/2009/jul/06/heidegger-philosophy-being; accessed April 22, 2010.

23. Ibid.

24. Concepts of anxiety have a complex history in Freudian thought that I cannot fully engage here. Freud understood anxiety as the effect of repressed sexuality, and then later "as a signal that a shock was coming. Trauma occurred when the anxiety signal failed." See Eli Zaretsky, *Secrets of the Soul: A Social and Cultural History of Psychoanalysis* (New York: Vintage Books), 125–26. Freud moves toward trauma to understand neuroses such as paranoia. Moreover, early formulations of anxiety understood it as a dread of castration. This view was modified to have to do with separation; the loss of the object that protects against harm causes anxiety (Zaretsky, *Secrets of the Soul,* 203). Anxiety was further revised by feminist analysts such as Karen Horney: "Anxiety was the awareness of a repressed impulse, the expression of which would involve an external danger. Anxiety arose from the frustration of any basic need, not just sexuality, and the extent to which a repressed impulse caused anxiety was 'largely dependent on the existing cultural attitude'" (Zaretsky, 210).

25. Sara Ahmed, *The Cultural Politics of Emotion* (New York: Routledge, 2004), 80n2.

26. Rachman, in Ahmed, *The Cultural Politics of Emotion,* 64.

27. Ahmed convincingly reads Frantz Fanon's violent misapprehension—"Look, a Negro"—in this way. See her chapter "The Affective Politics of Fear," in *The Cultural Politics of Emotion,* 62–81.

28. Russell Robinson, "Structural Dimensions of Romantic Preferences," *Fordham Law Review* 76 (2008): 2792.

29. Lauren Berlant, *The Female Complaint,* 13.

30. Dwight McBride, "It's a White Man's World."

31. Ahmed, *Cultural Politics,* 80n2.

32. See my longer discussion of this event in my essay "Ordinary Intersections," *Transforming Anthropology* 20, no. 1 (2012): 45–66.

33. See Phillip Brian Harper, "The Evidence of Felt Intuition: Minority Experience, Everyday Life, and Critical Speculative Knowledge," in *Black Queer Studies: A Critical Anthology,* ed. Mae Henderson and E. Patrick Johnson (Durham: Duke University Press, 2005), 106–23.

34. Marx, in Ben Anderson, "Affective Atmospheres," *Emotion, Space, and Society* 7 (2009): 77–81, 77.

35. Sianne Ngai, *Ugly Feelings*, 299.

36. For only one relevant example, consider Heather MacDonald's *National Review* article critiquing President Obama and Henry Louis Gates Jr.'s comments following the latter's arrest, "Promoting Racial Paranoia." http://www.nationalreview.com/articles/227946/promoting-racial-paranoia/heather-mac-donald, July 24, 2009; accessed June 13, 2010.

37. See B. Davin Stengel's interview with John L. Jackson, "Optimism and Paranoia." http://www.sas.upenn.edu/home/SASFrontiers/jackson.html, September 2008; accessed June 13, 2010.

38. John L. Jackson Jr., "Racial Paranoia vs. Race Cardology." http://anthromania.blogspot.com/2008/07/racial-paranoia-vs-race-cardology.html; accessed June 13, 2010.

39. From an interview, available at http://www.youtube.com/watch?v=nra5RTRRgAU; accessed June 13, 2010.

40. Russell Robinson, "Structural Dimensions of Romantic Preferences." For other depressing evidence of antiblack racism in online dating see, Kathryn Sweeney and Anne Borden, "Crossing the Line Online: Racial Preference of Internet Daters," *Marriage & Family Review* 45, nos. 6–8 (2009): 740–60; Cynthia Feliciano, Belinda Robnett, and Golnaz Komaie, "Gendered Racial Exclusion Among White Internet Daters," *Social Science Research* 38, no.1 (2009): 39–54; Glenn Tsunokai, Augustine Kposowa, and Michelle Adams, "Racial Preferences in Internet Dating: A Comparison of Four Birth Cohorts," *Western Journal of Black Studies* 33, no. 1 (2009): 1–15.

41. Ngai, *Ugly Feelings*, 398n3.

42. Michael Snediker, *Queer Optimism: Lyric Personhood and Other Felicitous Persuasions* (Minneapolis: University of Minnesota Press, 2009).

43. Ibid., 2.

44. See Nigel Thrift, *Non-Representational Theory* and José Muñoz, *Cruising Utopia*.

45. Giorgio Agamben, *The Open: Man and Animal*, trans. Kevin Attell (Stanford: Stanford University Press, 2004).

46. Kenji Yoshino, *Covering: The Hidden Assault on Our Civil Rights* (New York: Random House, 2006).

47. Fred Moten, "Black Optimism/Black Operations," conference paper, available online, http://lucian.uchicago.edu/blogs/politicalfeeling/resources-recourses/articles/; accessed March 13, 2010.

48. Ibid., 4.

49. Judith Halberstam, *The Queer Art of Failure* (Durham: Duke University Press), 11–12.

50. Snediker, 2.

51. See the collection of oral histories in the section "More than Mere Survival," in John Gwaltney's *Drylongso: A Self-Portrait of Black America* (New York: The New Press, 1993 [1980]).

52. Thrift, *Non-Representational Theory,* 20; see also Wright, *Drifting Toward Love.*

53. Bloch, in Thrift, 21.

54. Muñoz, 20.

CHAPTER FOUR. JUSTIN FUCKS THE FUTURE

1. Arun Saldanha, *Psychedelic White: Goa Trance and the Viscosity of Race* (Minneapolis: University of Minnesota Press, 2007), 7; my emphasis.

2. "Paula Zahn Now." http://transcripts.cnn.com/TRANSCRIPTS/0512/21/pzn.01.html; accessed March 30, 2011.

3. U.S. Department of Justice, Attorney General's Office, "Project Safe Childhood: Protecting Children from Online Exploitation and Abuse," May 2006.

4. See James Kincaid, *Child-Loving: The Erotic Child and Victorian Culture* (New York: Routledge, 1994) and *Erotic Innocence: The Culture of Child Molesting* (Durham: Duke University Press, 1998).

5. Kincaid, *Erotic Innocence,* 167.

6. In 2009, three Pennsylvania high school girls were threatened with arrest after semi-nude pictures of them were discovered on their classmates' cellphones. The girls and their mothers sued the county prosecutor after he threatened to bring child pornography charges against the girls. See Sean Hamill, "Students Sue Prosecutor in Cellphone Photos Case," *New York Times,* March 29, 2009. http://www.nytimes.com/2009/03/26/us/26sextext.html; accessed July 18, 2009. More recently, some eighth grade students in Washington State were arrested after circulating naked images of their peers. A plea was negotiated that allowed the children to avoid being prosecuted as child pornographers. In exchange, the students prepared educational materials on the dangers of sexting. See Jan Hoffman, "A Girl's Nude Photos, and Altered Lives," *New York Times,* March 26, 2011. http://www.nytimes.com/2011/03/27/us/27sexting.html?src=mv; accessed March 30, 2011.

7. Lee Edelman, *No Future: Queer Theory and the Death Drive* (Durham: Duke University Press, 2004).

8. Also see Lauren Berlant's discussions of "infantile citizenship" in her *The Queen of America Goes to Washington City: Essays on Sex and Citizenship* (Durham: Duke University Press, 1997).

9. Edelman, *No Future,* 2.

10. Ibid.

11. Ibid., 29.

12. Kurt Eichenwald, "Through His Webcam, a Boy Joins a Sordid Online World," *New York Times*, December 19, 2005. http://www.nytimes.com/2005/12/19/national/19kids.ready.html; accessed July 9, 2009.

13. I draw here both on my own reading of the *Times* articles, as well as on materials by Susie Bright and Debbie Nathan. See Susie Bright's blog posting, "When Kurt and Justin Met Debbie." http://susiebright.blogs.com/susie_brights_journal_/2007/09/once-upon-a-tim.html; accessed July 19, 2009. As my subsequent discussion will demonstrate, I also rely heavily on Debbie Nathan's reporting, "The New York Times, Kurt Eichenwald and the World of Justin Berry: Hysteria, Exploitation, and Witch Hunting In the Age of Internet Sex," *CounterPunch* nos. 7–8 (July 2007): 1–12.

14. Kurt Eichenwald, "Making a Connection with Justin," *New York Times*, December 19, 2005. http://www.nytimes.com/2005/12/19/business/19kidswebessay.html; accessed July 9, 2009.

15. Eichenwald, "Through His Webcam."

16. "The Young Boy Lured into Becoming an Internet Porn Star," the *Oprah Winfrey Show*, February 15, 2006. http://www.oprah.com/showinfo/The-Young-Boy-Lured-into-Becoming-an-Internet-Porn-Star_1; accessed July 9, 2009.

17. Bright, "When Kurt and Justin Met Debbie." I do not fully unpack this homophobic ick factor in this chapter. In brief, however, Bright's remark highlights the ways Berry's story articulates homophobic attitudes; it is not just the corruption of Berry's innocence that makes this scandal particularly salacious, but the ways this corruption is tied to anxieties about *homosexual* grooming. An earlier, sympathetic story about cam girls in *Salon* offers an important counterpoint. In this story, the girls are savvy young businesswomen, willing to trade a little skin or simply titillate in exchange for gifts. "Who's exploiting whom?" the article asks. Berry's sexuality is both more direct—he performed particular acts not just for gifts but money, and he also appeared to have been escorting—and deeply ambivalent. Although Eichenwald straight-washes him, emphasizing the fact that Berry initially got online to make new friends ("girls my age," he quotes him saying), Debbie Nathan's investigation reveals that Berry had had a sexual liaison with another teen and a man in his twenties when Berry was thirteen. And revealingly, in his Congressional testimony, Berry says that he had sex with prostitutes when he was sixteen; men, however, only ever molested him. The sex panic that accumulated in Berry's narrative thus depended on the particular hysterias that attend inter-generational queer sex—pederasty is hard to get behind—and fears about technology and sex. See Katherine Mieszkowski, "Candy from Strangers," Salon.com, August 13, 2001. http://dir.salon.com/tech/feature/2001/08/13/cam_girls/index.html; accessed July 9, 2009; Nathan, "The *New York Times*"; U.S. House of Representatives, "Sexual Exploitation of Children Over the

Internet: What Parents, Kids and Congress Need to Know about Child Predators," April 4, 2006, transcript.

18. "Paula Zahn Now,"

19. Melissa Block, "Story Unfolds of Minors and Web Camera Porn," *All Things Considered,* National Public Radio, January 2, 2006. http://www.npr.org/templates/transcript/transcript.php?storyId=5079510; accessed July 9, 2009.

20. "Web of Evil." http://sixtyminutes.ninemsn.com.au/article.aspx?id=295672, Sunday September16, 2007; accessed July 9, 2009.

21. National Center for Missing & Exploited Children, "Statistics," www.missingkids.com/en_US/.../CyberTiplineFactSheet.pdf; accessed July 23, 2009.

22. See Jack Shafer, "The *New York Times* Legal Aid Society." http://www.slate.com/articles/news_and_politics/press_box/2005/12/the_new_york_times_legal_aid_society.html, Slate.com, December 19, 2005; accessed July 23, 2009.

23. See the public editor column by Byron Calume, "Money, a Source and New Questions about a Story," *New York Times,* March 25, 2007. http://www.nytimes.com/2007/03/25/opinion/25pubed.html?_r=0; accessed July 23, 2009.

24. As I note below this story is not longer available but can be found at http://groups.google.com/group/alt.activism.children/browse_frm/thread/78ed686336161d3a/9a82b3af78f63040?lnk=raot&hl=en#9a82b3af78f63040.

25. Nathan, "Why I Need to See Child Porn," http://groups.google.com/group/alt.activism.children/browse_frm/thread/78ed686336161d3a/9a82b3af78f63040?lnk=raot&hl=en#9a82b3af78f63040.

26. Amy Adler, "The Perverse Law of Child Pornography," *Columbia Law Review* 209 (2001): 2–87.

27. Philip Jenkins, *Beyond Tolerance: Child Pornography on the Internet* (New York: New York University Press, 2001).

28. Kurt Eichenwald, "With Child Sex Sites on the Run, Nearly Nude Photos Hit the Web," *New York Times,* August 20, 2006; accessed July 23, 2009.

29. Bright, "When Kurt and Justin Met Debbie."

30. Ibid. The code can be found at http://www.law.cornell.edu/uscode/html/uscode18/usc_sec_18_00002252----000-.html. The affirmative defense reads, "It shall be an affirmative defense to a charge of violating paragraph (4) of subsection (a) that the defendant—

(1) possessed less than three matters containing any visual depiction proscribed by that paragraph; and

(2) promptly and in good faith, and without retaining or allowing any person, other than a law enforcement agency, to access any visual depiction or copy thereof—

(A) took reasonable steps to destroy each such visual depiction; or

(B) reported the matter to a law enforcement agency and afforded that agency access to each such visual depiction."

31. I am referring here to another moral panic, one that had, perhaps coincidentally, faltered by the late 1990s just as the hysteria surrounding children and the Internet began to wax. In the 1980s, widespread claims that children were suffering ritualized Satanic abuse spread, a combination of urban folklore and shady therapeutic methods that sought to recover suppressed memories. Nathan, alongside other journalists and academics, proved the accounts to be false.

32. Nathan, "The *New York Times,*" 9.

33. Carl Bialik, "Online Warnings Mean Well, but the Numbers Don't Add Up," *Wall Street Journal*, January 21, 2005. http://online.wsj.com/public/article/SB110617073758830511.html#READERSRESPOND; accessed May 17, 2011.

34. This report deserves a more nuanced unpacking than I provide here. But very briefly, note that finding unwanted sexual material was not necessarily upsetting to youth, that sexual solicitation could often occur among youth peer groups (especially when youth used the Internet with one another), and only a minority of youth reported being distressed by harassment or solicitation. Of course, even as the data in this report, like the earlier one, appear to have been conducted responsibly, the close relationship between the researchers and government agencies bears scrutiny. David Finkelhor, one of the authors of both reports and a key recipient of research monies to investigate online victimization himself, notes in the Internet Caucus Advisory Committee transcript the ways this data can be misappropriated. See "Just the Facts about Online Youth Victimization: Researchers Present the Facts and Debunk the Myths," Internet Caucus Advisory Committee, May 3, 2007, transcript. www.netcaucus.org/events/2007/youth/20070503transcript.pdf; accessed June 30, 2009. See also Janis Wolak, Kimberly Mitchell, and David Finkelhor, "Online Victimization of Youth: Five Years Later," National Center for Missing and Exploited Children, 2006. www.unh.edu/ccrc/pdf/CV138.pdf; accessed May 24, 2011.

35. Carl Bialik, "Measuring the Child Porn Trade," *Wall Street Journal,* April 16, 2006. http://online.wsj.com/public/article/SB114485422875624000-_UhifBvDF9HoRikGJZ_NWQxUYe0_20070417.html?mod=blogs; accessed May 17, 2011; Daniel Radosh, "How Big is the Online Kiddie Porn Industry?" Radosh.net, April 5, 2006. http://www.radosh.net/archive/001481.html; accessed May 17, 2011.

36. Dan Ackman, "How Big is Porn?" *Forbes,* May 25, 2001. http://www.forbes.com/2001/05/25/0524porn.html; accessed July 23, 2009. Estimates of commercial pornography take into account data supplied by the industry itself rather than independent resources. As Ackman points out, the industry is in the business of exaggerating scale.

37. Gregory Donovan "Whose Safety, Whose Security? Situating Young People in Cyberspace," 2008, unpublished manuscript.

38. Donovan: "According to Kathryn Montgomery the former director of the Center for Media Education which helped pass the previously discussed

COPPA, the abbreviations of these acts, CPPA and COPA, were purposely constructed to emulate COPPA and thus obfuscate their objectives within the public imagination," 10.

39. Internet Caucus Advisory Committee, "Just the Facts."

40. Lauren Berlant, "Cruel Optimism," *differences: A Journal of Feminist Cultural Studies* 17, no. 3 (2006): 20–36.

CHAPTER FIVE. THE *ÉLAN VITAL* OF DIY PORN

1. Pamela Paul, *Pornified: How Pornography is Transforming Our Lives, Our Relationships, and Our Families* (New York: Times Books, 2005).

2. Henri Bergson, "The Metaphysics of Life," trans. Michael Vaughan, *SubStance* 36, no. 3 (2007): 16–17.

3. Michael Vaughan, "Henri Bergson's *Creative Evolution*" *SubStance* 36, no. 3 (2007): 5.

4. Eugenie Brinkema, "A Title Does Not Ask, but Demands That You Make a Choice: On the Otherwise Films of Bruce LaBruce," *Criticism* 48, no. 1 (2007): 95–126.

5. Katrien Jacobs, *Netporn: DIY Web Culture and Sexual Politics* (Lanham, MD: Rowman and Littlefield, 2007).

6. Ibid., 2.

7. Ibid.

8. Ibid.

9. See, for example, Martin Meeker, *Contacts Desired: Gay and Lesbian Communications and Community, 1940s–1970s* (Chicago: University of Chicago Press, 2006).

10. Thomas Waugh, *Hard to Imagine: Gay Male Eroticism in Photography and Film from their Beginnings to Stonewall* (New York: Columbia University Press, 1996).

11. Many of the artists whose work entered into pornographic circulation, whether they were coded as art or as increasingly obvious physique culture erotica, were self-trained. Even those who received formal training exhibited the sort of DIY ethos that would make Martha Stewart and Bob Villa proud. One of the more original contributors to beefcake magazines, for example, James Bidgood, created elaborate sets in his New York City apartment and designed the gauzy clothing his models wore, in addition to lighting and photographing the scenes. For his cult film *Pink Narcissus*, Bidgood likewise shot the film and made the sets and costumes; in one scene, dreamy protagonist Bobby Kendall has a sexual encounter with a biker in a public toilet. Everything on screen, including the urinals and the motorcycle the biker walks in with, Bidgood made from scratch in the space of his apartment. See also Jim Tushinski's *That Man,* a documentary about Peter Berlin, who likewise took a DIY approach to creating an elaborate sexual persona

and photographing himself; Berlin enjoyed modest financial success through his lively mail-order business.

12. The introduction of video by the late 1970s and early 1980s transformed the American sexual landscape. Porn disappeared from Main Street and entered the American home. While gay men's participation in public sexual cultures such as theaters, video arcades, and bars, in which pornography played an important role, continued on into the 1980s (indeed, my own research argues that it has never entirely disappeared), the HIV/AIDS pandemic and the moral panics that accompanied it, along with urban redevelopment, also subjected these spaces to increasing surveillance and control. The net result has seen the diminishment of these spaces, spaces some critics have identified as essential not just to the vitality of gay male sexual cultures, but to democratic social life more generally (see esp. Delany 1999 and Warner 1999).

13. The Athletic Model Guild (AMG) of the 1950s and '60s represented a prototypical porn assembly line. AMG recruited hundreds of straight and gay models, photographing and filming the young men in a range of suggestive, erotically charged, but not hardcore, scenes.

14. See, among others, Christopher Kendall and Rus Funk, "Gay Male Pornography's 'Actors': When Fantasy Isn't," *Journal of Trauma Practice* 2, nos. 3/4: 93–114.

15. This literature is expansive, and as my arguments in the previous chapter indicated, I am deeply skeptical of the assumptions underlying many of these studies and the methods used to draw their conclusions. Many, I suggest, are circular, beginning and ending with the notion that any conjunction with "youth" and "sexuality" is inherently problematic. For recent academic examples, see Michael Flood, "The Harms of Pornography Exposure Among Children and Young People," *Child Abuse Review* 18, no. 6 (2009): 384–400; Michael Twohig, Jesse Crosby, and Jared Cox, "Viewing Internet Pornography: For Whom is it Problematic, How, and Why?" *Sexual Addiction & Compulsivity* 16, no. 4 (2009): 253–66; and Colleen Bryant, "Adolescence, Pornography, and Harm," *Youth Studies Australia* 29, no. 1 (2010): 18–26. For more ordinary ones, simply type "porn" and "youth" into an Internet search engine.

16. Although some anti-porn feminists adeptly expose the ties that bind patriarchy to capitalism and sexual exploitation, their commitment to a very narrowly defined "radical" feminism produces an equally narrow intellectual and political imagination. Anti-porn feminists argue that pornography reflects and thereby reproduces violence against women. The sexual images of porn achieve their force through misogynist humiliation and degradation; they show and become harm. In their view, women involved in pornography's production are abused and exploited before they appear on screen (in the form of childhood abuse or prostitution), behind the scenes, and then again on screen. These views have been subjected to extensive critique, generating a schism among many feminists. Some feminists have responded to the claims

of Dworkin, MacKinnon, and other anti-porn feminists, arguing that while a critique of sexual violence is essential to feminist politics, the anti-porn stance goes much too far by incorrectly labeling all sexual representations as the same and by denying women the ability to express their sexuality, paradoxically disempowering the very people in whose name an anti-porn politics is waged. Although nearly all anti-porn feminists focus on heterosexual porn, they have also extended their radical critique to gay porn, which scholars like Kendall argue causes identical forms of harm as straight porn. In their view, all pornographic representations of sex are inherently inegalitarian and therefore unjust. Of course as a range of critics have pointed out, anti-porn feminists make many categorical, political, and material errors. They do not account for the diverse forms of pleasure people experience, ruling inegalitarian sex immoral. (One has to wonder what fully egalitarian sex looks like? Of course, within the feminist anti-porn schema such images are a priori out of bounds, because to represent sex is to reproduce injustice). My own perspective, as my commitment to porn's vitality should demonstrate, is adamantly pro-sex. These debates have a lengthy history, but for one vital source relevant to these debates, see Linda Williams, *Hard Core: Power, Pleasure, and the Frenzy of the Visible* (Berkeley: University of California Press,1999) (see especially her supplemental bibliographies).

17. Jacobs, *Netporn,* 49.

18. Feona Attwood, "No Money Shot? Commerce, Pornography, and New Sex Taste Cultures," *Sexualities* 10, no. 4 (2007): 441–56.

19. Peter Lehman, "You and Voyeurweb: Illustrating the Shifting Representation of the Penis on the Internet with User-Generated Content," *Cinema Journal* 46, no. 4 (2007): 108–16, 111.

20. Ibid.

21. Ibid., 112.

22. Williams, *Hard Core.*

23. Stephen Maddison and Sharif Mowlabocus usefully point out some limits to notions of sexual or pornographic "freedom." Freedom does not refer to the absence of all constraints, but rather refers to particular relationships to forms of authority. In Maddison's argument, powerful cultural myths about the emancipatory qualities of sexual liberalism, viz., porn often obscure the forms of self-management and regulation, and commercial acquisitions, necessary to achieve sexual freedom. Mowlabocus's argument focuses on XTube amateurs and emphasizes the forms of immaterial labor that go into producing oneself as an autonomous, and entrepreneurial, sexual agent. See Stephen Maddison, "Online Obscenity and Myths of Freedom," in *Porn.com: Making Sense of Online Pornography,* ed. Feona Attwood (New York: Peter Lang, 2010), 17–33; and Sharif Mowlabocus, "Porn 2.0? Technology, Social Practice, and the New Online Porn Industry" in *Porn.com,* 69–87.

24. Atwood, "No Money Shot?," 443.

25. Barcan, in ibid., 448.

26. Messina, in ibid.

27. See especially Waugh, *Hard to Imagine.*

28. For important exceptions, see some of the work of director Wash West, including *The Hole.* See also the work of Bruce LaBruce, who fuses experimental, political, and pornographic filmmaking. Two dramatic Web series with explicit content have recently emerged, Channel 1's "Raising the Bar" and NakedSword's "Golden Gate."

29. According to TLA, a leading retailer of gay DVDs, none of the top ten best-selling videos of 2010 were narrative features (instead, they featured twincest, barebacking, and watersports!). See http://www.tlavideo.com/gay-top-selling-gay-adult-titles-of-2010/feature-8634-3 and http://thesword.com/index.php/all-stories/42-depts/4151-incest-bareback-and-watersports-movies-were-top-selling-titles-of-2010.html.

30. Specialty or fetish videos, spanking or pissplay, to take two examples, vary only in their emphasis of certain acts.

31. I do not address sound, although it's clearly important whether there's an emphasis in natural sound, the voice, no sound, or, as in The Black Spark's videos, musical soundtracks.

32. For a compelling reading of semen in DIY straight porn, see Lisa Jean Moore and Juliana Weissbein, "Cocktail Parties: Fetishizing Semen in Pornography Beyond *Bukkake,*" in *Everyday Pornography,* ed. Karen Boyle (New York: Routledge, 2010), 77–89.

33. The suggestion of a backstory is made evident on The Black Spark's profile page on XTube as well. Under the categories "Turn Ons" and "Turn Offs," for example, are listed "you" and "him," respectively.

34. Jane Ward, "Dude Sex: White Masculinities and 'Authentic' Heterosexuality Among Dudes Who Have Sex With Dudes," *Sexualities* 11, no. 4 (2008): 414–34.

35. Atwood, "No Money Shot?," 449–50.

36. Tatiana Bazzichelli and Gaia Novati, "Concept." http://www.cum-2cut.net/en/index.php?sect=concept; accessed December 24, 2010.

37. "Pr0n" is hacker slang for porn. The pr0n competition at CUM-2CUT makes the technology the protagonist: "People have to deal with pornography using media or creating digital codes or any other video projects. There is no limits [*sic*] to the possible uses/derivations of technology. The real limits to cross are only the sexual stereotypes." http://www.cum2cut.net/en/index.php?sect=pron; accessed December 24, 2010.

38. Tatiana Bazzichelli, "On Hactivist Pornography and Networked Porn," unpublished manuscript available online.

39. Ibid., 4.

40. Ibid.; my emphasis.

41. Ibid., 8.

42. Bergson, in Monica Greco, "On the Vitality of Vitalism," *Theory, Culture & Society* 22, no. 1 (2005): 18.

43. Bergson, "The Metaphysics of Life," 29.

CODA

1. Patrick Keilty, "The Social and Embodied Arrangements of Online Pornography," unpublished manuscript (2010).

2. Sherry Turkle, *Alone Together: Why We Expect More from Technology and Less From Each Other* (New York: Basic Books, 2011), 38.

3. See Mark Coté and Jennifer Pybus, "Learning to Immaterial Labour 2.0: MySpace and Social Networks," *ephemera: theory and politics in organization* 7, no. 1 (2007): 88–106.

4. Sharif Mowlabocus, "Porn 2.0? Technology, Social Practice, and the New Online Porn Industry," in *Porn.com: Making Sense of Online Pornography*, ed. Feona Attwood, (New York: Peter Lang, 2010), 69–87.

5. Coté and Pybus, in Mowlabocus, "Porn 2.0?," 80.

6. Douchebags of Grindr thus shares some similarities with "revenge porn" sites such as the now-defunct *Is Anyone Up?*, to which users submitted sexually explicit images of exes, band members, or random people with whom they interacted online. These sexual snapshots were typically paired with screenshots of the subject's Facebook page.

7. Jay Bolter and Richard Grusin, *Remediation: Understanding New Media* (Cambridge: MIT Press, 1999).

8. Mary Gray, *Out in the Country: Youth, Media, and Queer Visibility in Rural America* (New York: New York University Press, 2009), 17.

9. Eugene Thacker, *Biomedia* (Minneapolis: University of Minnesota Press, 2004), 11.

10. Patrick Keilty, "The Social and Embodied Arrangements of Online Pornography" (2011), unpublished manuscript.

Bibliography

60 Minutes (Australia). 2007. "Web of Evil." Ninemsn, September 16, 2007. Accessed June 9, 2009. http://sixtyminutes.ninemsn.com/stories/liambartlett/295672/web-of-evil.

Ackman, Dan. "How Big is Porn?" *Forbes,* May 25, 2001.

Agamben, Giorgio. *The Open: Man and Animal.* Trans. Kevin Attell. Stanford: Stanford University Press, 2004.

Ahmed, Sara. *The Cultural Politics of Emotion.* New York: Routledge, 2004.

Allison, Anne. *Millennial Monsters: Japanese Toys and the Global Imagination.* Berkeley: University of California Press, 2006.

Anderson, Ben, and John Wylie. "On Geography and Materiality." *Environment and Planning A* 41 (2009): 318–35.

Armstrong, John. *Conditions of Love: The Philosophy of Intimacy.* New York: Norton, 2003.

Attwood, Feona. "No Money Shot? Commerce, Pornography, and New Sex Taste Cultures." *Sexualities* 10, no. 4 (2007): 441–56.

Bailey, Cameron. "Virtual Skin: Articulating Race in Cyberspace." In *Immersed in Technology: Art and Virtual Environments,* ed. Mary Ann Moser and Douglas MacLeod, 29–49. Cambridge: MIT Press, 1996.

Bataille, Georges. *The Tears of Eros.* Trans. Peter Connor. San Francisco: City Lights Books, 1989.

Bazzichelli, Tatiana. "On Hacktivist Pornography and Networked Porn." Accessed January 15, 2010. http://tinyurl.com/d4fofd9.

———, and Gaia Novati. "Concept." Accessed January 15, 2010. http://www.cum2cut.net/en/index.php?sect=concept.

———. "Pr0n." Accessed December 24, 2010. http://www.cum2cut.net/en/index.php?sect=pron.

BBC News. "Gay Rights Win in Warcraft World." Accessed December 4, 2012. News.bbc.co.uk/1/hi/technology/4700754.stm.

Bergson, Henri. "The Metaphysics of Life." *SubStance* 36, no. 3 (2007): 25–32.

Berlant, Lauren. *Cruel Optimism*. Durham: Duke University Press, 2011.

———. *The Female Complaint: The Unfinished Business of Sentimentality in American Culture*. Durham: Duke University Press, 2008.

———. *The Queen of America Goes to Washington City: Essays on Sex and Citizenship*. Series Q. Durham: Duke University Press, 1997.

Berlant, Lauren, ed. *Intimacy*. Chicago: University of Chicago Press, 2000.

Bialik, Carl. "Measuring the Child Porn Trade." *Wall Street Journal*, April 16, 2006. Accessed May 17, 2011. http://online.wsj.com/public/article/SB114485422875624000-_UhifBvDF9HoRikGJZ_NWQx-UYe0_20070417.html?mod=blogs.

———. 2005. "Online Warnings Mean Well, but the Numbers Don't Add Up." *Wall Street Journal*, January 1, 2005. Accessed May 17, 2011. http://online.wsj.com/public/article/SB110617073758830511.html#READERSRESPOND.

Block, Melissa. "Story Unfolds of Minors and Web Camera Porn." National Public Radio, January 2, 2006. Accessed July 9, 2009. http://www.npr.org/templates/transcript/transcript.php?storyId=5079510.

Boellstorff, Tom. *Coming of Age in Second Life: An Anthropologist Explores the Virtually Human*. Princeton: Princeton University Press, 2008.

Bolter, Jay, and Richard Grusin. *Remediation: Understanding New Media*. Cambridge: MIT Press, 1999.

Bright, Susie. "When Kurt and Justin Met Debbie." Susie Bright's Journal, September 27, 2007. Accessed July 9, 2009. http://susiebright.blogs.com/susie_brights_journal_/2007/09/once-upon-a-tim.html.

Brinkema, Eugenia. "A Title Does Not Ask, but Demands that You make a Choice: On the Otherwise Films of Bruce LaBruce." *Criticism* 48, no. 1 (2007): 95–126.

Brooks, David. "The Alpha Geeks." *The New York Times,* May 22, 2008.

Bryant, Colleen. "Adolescence, Pornography, and Harm." *Youth Studies Australia* 29, no. 1 (2010): 18–26.

Bush, George W. "Project Safe Childhood: Protecting Children from Online Exploitation and Abuse." 2006. Web document no longer available.

Calume, Byron. "Money, a Source and New Questions about a Story." *New York Times,* March 25, 2007.

Castells, Manuel. *The Power of Identity*. Malden, MA: Blackwell, 2004.

Castronova, Edward. *Synthetic Worlds: The Business and Culture of Online Games*. Chicago: University of Chicago Press, 2005.

Chauncey, George. *Gay New York: Gender, Urban Culture, and the Makings of the Gay Male World, 1890–1940*. New York: Basic Books, 1994.

————. *Why Marriage? The History Shaping Today's Debate Over Gay Equality.* New York: Basic Books, 2005.

Colter, Ephen Glenn, and Dangerous Bedfellows, eds. *Policing Public Sex: Queer Politics and the Future of AIDS Activism.* Boston: South End Press, 1996.

Coté, Mark, and JenniferL Pybus. "Learning to Immaterial Labor 2.0: MySpace and Social Networks." *ephemera: theory and politics in organization* 7, no. 1 (2007): 88–106.

Critchley, Simon. "Being and Time Part 5: Anxiety." *The Guardian,* July 6, 2009.

Cvetkovich, Ann. *An Archive of Feelings: Trauma, Sexuality, and Lesbian Public Cultures.* Durham: Duke University Press, 2003.

Dean, Jodi. *Democracy and Other Neoliberal Fantasies: Communicative Capitalism and Left Politics.* Durham: Duke University Press, 2009.

Delany, Samuel R. *Times Square Red, Times Square Blue. Sexual Cultures.* New York: New York University Press, 1999.

Deleuze, Gilles. "Immanence: A Life." In *Pure Immanence: Essays on a Life,* trans. Anne Boyman, 25–33. New York: Zone Books, 2001.

D'Emilio, John, and Esther Freedman. *Intimate Matters: A History of Sexuality in America.* New York: Basic Books, 1994.

Donovan, Gregory. "Whose Safety, Whose Security? Situating Young People in Cyberspace." Unpublished essay.

Duggan, Lisa. *The Twilight of Equality: Neoliberalism, Cultural Politics, and the Attack on Democracy.* Boston: Beacon Press, 2003.

Edelman, Lee. *No Future: Queer Theory and the Death Drive.* Durham: Duke University Press, 2004.

Eichenwald, Kurt. "Making a Connection with Justin." *New York Times,* December 19, 2005.

————. "Through His Webcam, A Boy Joins a Sordid Online World." *New York Times,* December 19, 2005.

Eng, David L., and David Kazanjian. *Loss: The Politics of Mourning.* Berkeley: University of California Press, 2003.

"Feel Tank Manifesto." No longer available. Accessed June 17, 2010. http://feeltankchicago.net/.

Feliciano, Cynthia, Belinda Robnett, and Golnaz Komaie. "Gendered Racial Exclusion among White Internet Daters." *Social Science Research* 38, no. 1 (2009): 39–54.

Fisher, Phillip. *The Vehement Passions.* Princeton: Princeton University Press, 2002.

Flood, Michael. "The Harms of Pornography Exposure among Children and Young People." *Child Abuse Review* 18, no. 6 (2009): 384–400.

Galloway, Alexander. "Networks." In *Critical Terms for Media Studies,* eds. W. J. T. Mitchell and Mark B. N. Hansen, 280–96. Chicago: University of Chicago Press, 2010.

Gordon, Avery. *Ghostly Matters: Haunting and the Sociological Imagination.* Minneapolis: University of Minnesota Press, 1997.

Gosine, Andil. "Brown to Blonde at Gay.Com: Passing White in Queer Cyberspace." In *Queer Online: Media Technology and Society,* eds. Kate O'Riordan and David Phillips, 139–53. New York: Peter Lang, 2007.

Gray, Mary. *Out in the Country: Youth, Media, and Queer Visibility in Rural America.* New York: New York University Press, 2009.

Greco, Monica. "On the Vitality of Vitalism." *Theory, Culture & Society* 22, no. 1 (2005): 15–27.

Gregg, Melissa. "A Mundane Voice." *Cultural Studies* 18, no. 2/3 (2004): 363–83.

Gwaltney, John. *Drylongso.* New York: The Free Press, 1993.

Halberstam, Judith. *In a Queer Time and Place: Transgender Bodies, Subcultural Lives.* New York: New York University Press, 2005.

———. *The Queer Art of Failure.* Durham: Duke University Press, 2011.

Hamill, Sean. "Students Sue Prosecutor in Cellphone Photos Case." *New York Times,* March 29, 2009.

Haraway, Donna Jeanne. *Modest_Witness@SecondMillenium. FemaleMan_Meets_OncoMouse: Feminism and Technoscience.* New York: Routledge, 1997.

Harper, Phillip Brian. "The Evidence of Felt Intuition: Minority Experience, Everyday Life, and Critical Speculative Knowledge." In *Black Queer Studies: A Critical Anthology,* eds. E. Patrick Johnson and Mae Henderson, 106–23. Durham: Duke University Press, 2005.

Henery, Celeste. "The Balance of Souls: Self-Making and Mental Wellness in the Lives of Aging Black Women in Brazil." PhD diss, University of Texas–Austin, 2010.

Higgs, David, ed. *Queer Sites: Gay Urban Histories since 1600.* New York: Routledge, 1999.

Hoad, Neville Wallace. *African Intimacies: Race, Homosexuality, and Globalization.* Minneapolis: University of Minnesota Press, 2007.

Holland, Sharon. *Raising the Dead: Readings in Death and Black Subjectivity.* Durham: Duke University Press, 2000.

Humphreys, Laud. "Tearoom Trade." In *Public Sex / Gay Space,* ed. William Leap, 29–54. New York: Columbia University Press, 1999.

Internet Caucus Advisory Committee. "Just the Facts about Online Youth Victimization: Researchers Present the Facts and Debunk the Myths." Netcaucus.org, May 3, 2007. Transcript. Accessed June 30, 2009. http://www.netcaucus.org/events/2007/youth/.

Jackson, John L. "John L. Jackson Jr. on 'Racial Paranoia.'" YouTube.com. Accessed June 13, 2010. http://www.youtube.com/watch?v=nra5RTRRgAU.

———. *Real Black: Adventures in Racial Sincerity.* Durham: Duke University Press, 2005.

Jacobs, Katrien. *Netporn : DIY Web Culture and Sexual Politics.* Lanham, MD: Rowman and Littlefield, 2007.

Jenkins, Henry. *Convergence Culture: Where Old and New Media Collide.* New York: New York University Press, 2006.

Jenkins, Philip. *Beyond Tolerance: Child Pornography on the Internet.* New York: New York University Press, 2001.

Johnson, E. Patrick. *Appropriating Blackness: Performance and the Politics of Authenticity.* Durham: Duke University Press, 2003.

Keilty, Patrick. "The Social and Embodied Arrangements of Online Pornography." Unpublished essay.

Kendall, Christopher N., and Rus Ervin Funk. "Gay Male Pornography's 'Actors': When Fantasy Isn't." *Journal of Trauma Practice* 2, no. 3/4 (2003): 93–114.

Kincaid, James. *Child-Loving: The Erotic Child and Victorian Culture.* New York: Routledge, 1994.

———. *Erotic Innocence: The Culture of Child Molesting.* Durham: Duke University Press, 1998.

Kolko, Beth E., Lisa Nakamura, and Gilbert B. Rodman, eds. *Race in Cyberspace.* New York: Routledge, 1999.

KXAN News. "Sex, Parks and Videotape." Accessed January 14, 2007. http://www.kxan.com/Global/story.asp?S=4464515.

Lamb, Gregory M. "Are Multiplayer Online Games More Addictive?" *USA Today,* October 12, 2005. Accessed December 8, 2012. www.usatoday.com/tech/gaming/2005-10-12-mmorpgs-addictive_x.htm.

Leap, William. *Public Sex/Gay Space.* New York: Columbia University Press, 1999.

Lehman, Peter. "You and Voyeurweb: Illustrating the Shifting Representation of the Penis on the Internet with User-Generated Content." *Cinema Journal* 46, no. 4 (2007): 108–16.

Lorimer, Hayden. "Cultural Geography: The Busyness of being More-than-Representational." *Progress in Human Geography* 29, no. 1 (2005): 83–94.

MacDonald, Heather. "Promoting Racial Paranoia." *National Review,* July 2009.

Maddison, Stephen. "Online Obscenity and Myths of Freedom." In *Porn.Com: Making Sense of Online Pornography,* ed. Feona Attwood, 17–33. New York: Peter Lang, 2010.

Massumi, Brian. *Parables for the Virtual: Movement, Affect, Sensation.* Durham: Duke University Press, 2002.

McBride, Dwight. "It's a White Man's World." In *Why I Hate Abercrombie and Fitch,* 88–131. New York: New York University Press, 2005.

McGlotten, Shaka. "Ordinary Intersections: Speculations on Difference, Justice, and Utopia in Black Queer Life." *Transforming Anthropology* 20, no. 1 (2012): 123–37.

———. 2007. "Virtual Intimacies: Love, Addiction, and Identity @ the Matrix." In *Queer Online: Media Technology and Society,* ed. Kate O'Riordan and David Phillips, 123–37. New York: Peter Lang, 2012.

Meeker, Martin. *Contacts Desired: Gay and Lesbian Communications and Community, 1940s–1970s.* Chicago: University of Chicago Press, 2006.

Mieszkowski, Katherine. "Candy from Strangers." Salon.com. Accessed July 9, 2009. http://dir.salon.com/tech/feature/2001/08/13/cam_girls/index.html.

Miller, Neil. *Sex Crime Panic: A Journey into the Paranoid Heart of the 1950s.* Los Angeles: Alyson Books, 2002.

Milne, Esther. "Email and Epistolary Technologies: Presence, Intimacy, Disembodiment." *Fibreculture* 2 (2012). Accessed December 1, 2012. http://two.fibreculturejournal.org/fcj-010-email-and-epistolary-technologies-presence-intimacy-disembodiment/.

Moore, Lisa Jean, and Juliana Weissbein. "Cocktail Parties: Fetishizing Semen in Pornography Beyond Bukkake." In *Everyday Pornography,* ed. Karen Boyle, 77–89. New York and London: Routledge, 2010.

Moten, Fred. "Black Optimism/Black Operations." Web.

Mowlabocus, Sharif. "Porn 2.0? Technology, Social Practice, and the New Online Porn Industry." In *Porn.Com: Making Sense of Online Pornography,* ed. Feona Attwood, 69–87. New York: Peter Lang, 2010.

Muñoz, José Esteban. "Cruising the Toilet: LeRoi Jones/Amiri Baraka, Radical Black Traditions, and Queer Futurity." *GLQ: A Journal of Lesbian and Gay Studies* 13, no. 2–3 (2007): 353–67.

Nakamura, Lisa. *Cybertypes: Race, Ethnicity, and Identity on the Internet.* New York: Routledge, 2002.

Nathan, Debbie. "The New York Times, Kurt Eichenwald, and the World of Justin Berry: Hysteria, Exploitation, and Witch Hunting in the Age of Internet Sex." *CounterPunch,* July 2007.

National Center for Missing and Exploited Children. "Statistics." Original Web source no longer available.

Ngai, Sianne. "Animatedness." In *Ugly Feelings,* 89–125. Cambridge: Harvard University Press, 2005.

Pine, Jason. *The Art of Making Do in Naples.* Minneapolis: University of Minnesota Press, 2012.

Puar, Jasbir K. *Terrorist Assemblages: Homonationalism in Queer Times.* Durham: Duke University Press, 2007.

Radosh, Daniel. "How Big is the Online Kiddie Porn Industry?" Radosh.net, January 1, 2003. Accessed May 17, 2011. http://www.radosh.net/archive/001481.html.

Robinson, Marnia, and Gary Wilson. "Straight Men, Gay Porn, and Other Brain Map Mysteries." *Psychology Today,* February 3, 2010.

Robinson, Russell. "Structural Dimensions of Romantic Preferences." *Fordham Law Review* 76 (2008): 2787–2819.

Ross, Brian. "Foley's IM Exchange with Underage Page." ABC News. Accessed December 1, 2012. http://abcnews.go.com/WNT/BrianRoss/Story?id=2509586&page=3#.UMN7mehTObl.

Rubin, Gayle. "Thinking Sex: Notes for a Radical Theory of the Politics of Sexuality." In *The Gay and Lesbian Studies Reader*, eds. Henry Abelove, M. A. Barale, and D. M. Halperin, 3–44. New York: Routledge, 1993.

Saldanha, Arun. *Psychedelic White: Goa Trance and the Viscosity of Race*. Minneapolis: University of Minnesota Press, 2007.

Saylor, Steven. "Amethyst, Texas." In *Gay Hometowns*, ed. J. Preston, 119–35. New York: Plume, 1992.

Sedgwick, Eve Kosofsky. *Touching Feeling: Affect, Pedagogy, Performativity*. Durham: Duke University Press, 2003.

Shafer, Jack. "The *New York Times* Legal Aid Society." Slate.com, accessed July 29, 2009. http://www.slate.com/articles/news_and_politics/press_box/2005/12/the_new_york_times_legal_aid_society.html.

Shaviro, Steven. "Interstitial Life: Novelty and Double Causality in Kant, Whitehead, and Deleuze." www.shaviro.com/Othertexts/New.pdf.

Shields, Rob. *The Virtual*. New York: Routledge, 2003.

Shouse, Eric. "Feeling, Emotion, Affect." *M/C Journal* 8, no. 6 (2005). Accessed June 17, 2010. http://journal.media-culture.org.au/0512/03-shouse.php.

Sloan, Carrie. "Why are Geeks the New Chic?" MSNBC. Accessed December 4, 2012. www.msnbc.msn.com/id/22219377/.

Snediker, Michael. *Queer Optimism: Lyric Personhood and Other Felicitous Persuasions*. Minneapolis: University of Minnesota Press, 2009.

Stengel, B. D. "Optimism and Paranoia." University of Pennsylvania. Accessed 6/13, 2010. http://www.sas.upenn.edu/home/SASFrontiers/jackson.html.

Stewart, Kathleen. "On the Politics of Cultural Theory: A Case for 'Contaminated' Critique." *Social Research* 58, no. 2 (1991): 395–412.

———. *Ordinary Affects*. Durham: Duke University Press, 2007.

———. "Weak Theory in an Unfinished World." *Journal of Folklore Research* 45, no. 1 (2008): 71–82.

Stone, Allucquére Rosanne. *The War of Desire and Technology at the Close of the Mechanical Age*. Cambridge: MIT Press, 1995.

Sullivan, Andrew. *Virtually Normal*. New York: Vintage, 1996.

Sweeney, Kathryn, and Anne Borden. "Crossing the Line Online: Racial Preferences of Internet Daters." *Marriage and Family Review* 45, no. 6–8 (2009): 740–60.

Taylor, T. L. *Play between Worlds: Exploring Online Game Culture*. Cambridge: MIT Press, 2006.

Thacker, Eugene. *Biomedia*. Minneapolis: University of Minnesota Press, 2004.

The Oprah Winfrey Show. "The Young Boy Lured into Becoming an Internet Porn Star." February 15, 2006. Accessed July 9, 2009. http://www.oprah.com/showinfo/The-Young-Boy-Lured-into-Becoming-an-Internet-Porn-Star_1.

Thrift, Nigel. *Non-Representational Theory: Space|Politics|Affect*. New York: Routledge, 2008.

Tsunokai, Glenn, Augustine Kposowa, and Michelle Adams. "Racial Preferences in Internet Dating: A Comparison of Four Birth Cohorts." *Western Journal of Black Studies* 33, no. 1 (2009): 1–15.

Turkle, Sherry. *Alone Together: Why we Expect More from Technology and Less from each Other.* New York: Basic Books, 2011.

———.*Life on the Screen: Identity in the Age of the Internet.* New York: Simon and Schuster, 1995.

Twohig, Michael, Jesse Crosby, and Jared Cox. "Viewing Internet Pornography: For Whom is it Problematic, How, and Why?" *Sexual Addiction and Compulsivity* 16, no. 4 (2009): 253–66.

Tyler, Imogen, and Elena Loizidou. "The Promise of Lauren Berlant." *Cultural Values* 4, no. 3 (2000): 497–511.

U.S. House of Representatives. "Sexual Exploitation of Children Over the Internet: What Parents, Kids and Congress Need to Know about Child Predators," April 4, 2006. Transcript.

Vaid, Urvashi. *Virtual Equality.* New York: Anchor Books, 1995.

Vaughan, Michael. "Henri Bergson's *Creative Evolution.*" *SubStance* 36, no. 3 (2007): 7–24.

Ward, Jane. "Dude Sex: White Masculinities and 'Authentic' Heterosexuality among Dudes Who have Sex with Dudes." *Sexualities* 11, no. 4 (2008): 414–34.

Warner, Michael. *The Trouble with Normal: Sex, Politics, and the Ethics of Queer Life.* New York: The Free Press, 1999.

Waugh, Thomas. *Hard to Imagine: Gay Male Eroticism in Photography and Film from Their Beginnings to Stonewall.* New York: Columbia University Press, 1996.

Williams, Linda. *Hard Core: Power, Pleasure, and the "Frenzy of the Visible."* Berkeley: University of California Press, 1999.

Wolak, Janis, Kimberly Mitchell, and David Finkelhor. "Online Victimization of Youth: Five Years Later." National Center for Missing and Exploited Children, 2006. Accessed May 24, 2011. www.unh.edu/ccrc/pdf/CV138.pdf.

Wright, Kai. *Drifting Toward Love: Black, Brown, and Coming of Age on the Streets of New York.* Boston: Beacon Press, 2008.

Yoshino, Kenji. *Covering: The Hidden Assault on our Civil Rights.* New York: Random House, 2006.

Zahn, Paula. "Paula Zahn Now, Transcript." CNN.com. Accessed March 30, 2011. http://transcripts.cnn.com/TRANSCRIPTS/0512/21/pzn.01.html.

Zaretsky, Eli. *Secrets of the Soul: A Social and Cultural History of Psychoanalysis.* New York: Alfred A. Knopf, 2004.

Zittrain, Jonathan. *The Future of the Internet and How to Stop It.* New Haven: Yale University Press, 2008.

Index

Boellstorf, Tom, 46
Bolter, Jay, 130
Bryanterry, 109–112, 117
Bull Creek Park, 28, 29

Cadinot, Jean Daniel, 106
Cam4, 101
carnality, 1, 2, 9, 21, 26–27, 38, 123.
  See also intimacy
Chauncey, George, 137n3
Chester French, 113, 115
child pornography, 79–80, 83–94,
  97–99, 148n6, 153n15. *See also*
  Internet; pornography
Child, the, 13, 80–83, 91–92,
  97–98, 99. *See also* Edelman, Lee;
  reproductive futurism
Child Online Protection Act
  (COPA), 93–94, 152n38
Child Pornography Prevention Act
  (CPPA), 93, 152n38
Children's Internet Protection Act
  (CIPA), 93–94
Children's Online Privacy
  Protection Act (COPPA), 92–93,
  152n38
Cinema West, 24, 25
communicative capitalism, 10, 11
Congressional Internet Caucus
  Advisory Committee (CICAC),
  95
convergence culture, 14, 104
Coté, Mark, 127
Counterpunch, 86
Craig, Larry, 31–33
Creative Evolution (Bergson), 103
cruel optimism, 96, 100
cruising, 4, 5, 6, 17, 19, 24, 61, 70,
  73; and Grindr, 124–130, 133–134
CUM2CUT, 108, 118–119, 121–
  122
cyberspace, 2–3, 63, 93, 137n7

Dada, 121
Dean, Jodi, 10
Delany, Samuel, 4
Deleuze, Gilles, 1, 8, 60, 64; and
  Guattari, 8; virtuality, 8, 39. *See
  also* virtual
Donovan, Gregory, 93, 151n38
Douchebags of Grindr, 128–135
Dudesnude.com, 70

Edelman, Lee, 82–83, 91, 99–100
Eichenwald, Kurt, 79, 80, 81, 83–91,
  97, 98–99, 149n17
élan vital, 14, 102–104, 122
emotion. *See* affect
erotic innocence, 24, 80–81, 92, 96

failure: and intimacy, 7, 18, 19, 31,
  32, 33, 36–37, 59; as generative,
  75, 125; Judith Halberstam's
  concept of, 75; and racism, 71;
  and online cruising, 128; and
  redemption, 80, 96–97; and
  queer desire, 9; and sex in public,
  21, 23, 24, 27, 30, 34, 38; and
  virtuality, 2, 10, 27, 35, 37, 99,
  and *World of Warcraft*, 47, 48, 53,
  58
feelings. *See* affect
Finkelhor, David, 90, 95–96, 151n34
Fisher, Phillip, 64
Fluxus, 121
Foley, Mark, 31–34, 141n16
Freud, Sigmund, 67, 71, 146n24
*The Future of the Internet and How to
  Stop It* (Zittrain), 137n7
futurity, 60, 99

Galloway, Alexander, 5–6
gaming, 7, 39, 46, 55; See also *World
  of Warcraft*
Gay.com, 3, 56, 61, 129

Made in the USA
Middletown, DE
19 August 2015